Terrorism and Hostage Negotiations

Other Titles in This Series

Westview Special Studies in National and International Terrorism

Terrorism and Hostage Negotiations
Abraham H. Miller

How effective are the methods currently used to deal with hostage situations? This study attempts to answer that question by examining the ways in which terrorists manipulate the hostage/ barricade tactic--one of the most formidable and frightening devices in their arsenal--and by analyzing the response of law enforcement officers and policymakers to its use. Drawing on case materials and interviews with high-level decision makers, both in the United States and abroad, who are involved with domestic and international terrorist operations, Professor Miller analyzes the political and psychological motifs of hostage/barricade dramas. He then looks at terrorism, particularly political terrorism, within the broader theoretical context of the general study of political violence and the operational concerns of public decision makers and law enforcement personnel.

Abraham H. Miller is professor of political science at the University of Cincinnati. A specialist on political violence, in 1976 and 1977 he was a visiting fellow with the National Institute of Law Enforcement and Criminal Justice, U.S. Department of Justice.

Terrorism and Hostage Negotiations

Abraham H. Miller

Westview Press / Boulder, Colorado

*Westview Special Studies in National
and International Terrorism*

This research was supported by Grant Number 76-NI-99-0108
awarded by the National Institute of Law Enforcement and Criminal Justice of the Law Enforcement Assistance Administration,
United States Department of Justice, under the Omnibus Crime
Control and Safe Streets Act of 1968, as amended. Points of
view or opinions stated in this work are those of the author
and do not necessarily represent the official position or policies of the United States Department of Justice.

Published in 1980 in the United States of America by
     Westview Press, Inc.
     5500 Central Avenue
     Boulder, Colorado 80301
     Frederick A. Praeger, Publisher

Library of Congress Catalog Card Number: 79-3288
ISBN: 0-89158-856-6

Printed and bound in the United States of America.
Composition for this book was provided by the author.

Contents

Preface

In the 1976-1977 academic year, I was a visiting fellow with the National Institute of Law Enforcement and Criminal Justice, Law Enforcement Assistance Administration, U.S. Department of Justice, Washington, D.C. I came to Washington with a background in the study of political violence. I had written about the black urban riots,[1] the campus violence of the 1960's[2] and had explored some of the theoretical issues related to the development of a theory of political violence.[3] Consequently, my incursion into the elusive and exciting topic of terrorism and hostage negotiations began with an academic mind-set formed by some of this earlier work. There was a problem. Hostages were being taken, a barricade situation would ensue and officials would have to decide if and how to negotiate. Across the broad international landscape, most such situations are acted out by political terrorists, but within the continental United States, such situations generally ensue in the course of interrupted felonies, where the motivation to seize hostages and the method of operation are quite different from those encountered in a political terrorist situation. All such episodes leave data. As there are often some regularities in similar kinds of human behavior, even under diverse circumstances, part of the explanation of how to deal with such situations could perhaps be ferreted out from the kinds of data entwined in these episodes.

My inclination was to perceive the problem of what to do in response to a hostage situation through the intellectual prism wrought by years of training as a social scientist. Each event could be taken as a series of data pieces, broken apart into a number of critical variables and dissected.

The field of variables could then be aggregated across events, terrorist groups, and modes of responses of social control agents to present a probabilistic set of statements about what responses work under what circumstances.

I still have a lot of confidence in that methodology and believe the study of terrorism both for theoretical and operational concerns would be greatly enriched by a commitment of resources to this type of undertaking. It soon became apparent, however, that such a project went far beyond the time and resources available to me as an individual researcher within the context of the fellowship project. Two additional things were also relevant to the ultimate conceptualization of how the research was conducted. One was that Edward Mickolus, of the Central Intelligence Agency, had already undertaken this type of approach to the study of terrorism. Although we possessed some critical differences in orientation and perspective, I saw no point in duplicating Mickolus' work. Also, Mickolus, through the good offices of the Inter-University Consortium for Political Research, had made available to me the first batch of his machine-readable data. Despite insightful conceptualization, assiduous work, and coverage of a broad range of sources, Mickolus' file, "Project Iterate," at least in its initial form, contained too much missing data to provide the analytical coverage that was intrinsic to my own investigations. The file did contain excellent descriptive information and enriched my research, and I am grateful for having had access to it. However, its use was largely restricted, because of the missing data problems, to rather general types of descriptions. Analyses of specific groups were quite limited for this reason. A greater commitment to resources and access to the foreign language press would have greatly enhanced the utility inherent in the Mickolus project. Hopefully, the utility of Mickolus' design will achieve sufficient recognition at some point to obtain the resources it richly deserves.

There was yet a second reason for the change in orientation toward the research. This resulted from learning that the police had acquired a great deal of information about hostage situations and had developed some special programs to deal with them. Although virtually all of the experience the police had acquired had been the result of encounters with ordinary felons and not with political terrorists, the resulting methods were ones that would ultimately be used in situations that required negotiations with political terrorists. How effective were these methods? What reasonable implications could be deduced from them for political terrorist situations? As the answers to these questions were not generally known or even pursued on a national basis, it seemed that this would be a more appropriate course of inquiry. Moreover, by further pursuing these questions in the international context, an even broader frame of reference could be created against which the questions could be entertained.

Through contacts with representatives of foreign governments and law enforcement agencies and through investigations of the literature on terrorism, I attempted to put my initial questions about hostage negotiations in this broader perspective. Much of my research is built on in-depth analysis of specific cases and the subjective interpretations of law enforcement personnel and government officials. Had I been able to obtain in-depth case analyses and first-hand accounts of other hostage episodes, my interpretations and conclusions would perhaps have been somewhat different. Experienced law enforcement officers who work in hostage negotiations note that every case is distinctly unique. Sometimes a good negotiation goes sour and one that appears to be poorly nurtured ends in capitulation. On the other hand, the same people know that certain procedures do work, or at least have a high probability of success. Although, the scenario of hostage negotiations is like all human behavior inasmuch as it follows certain probabilistic outcomes, the outcome of any specific situation is unique.

I have tried to assess these procedures and their implications for dealing with political terrorists. It should be remembered that political terrorism specifically, within the context of any individual terrorist movement, and political terrorism generally is constantly changing. The suggestions and interpretations which I have drawn from my research about hostage negotiations may or may not be applicable if certain changes come about. I nonetheless believe my observations are sufficiently grounded in data as to be at least suggestive of the circumstances under which they will or will not be applicable and why. Knowing this, the research might also be of value in stimulating concerns about alternative modes of operations.

One of the concerns I encountered in my travels

and discussions with law enforcement and government officials both here and abroad is the strong desire on the part of all of them, but especially those at the lower ranks, to know more about the experiences that their fellow officers have had in dealing with hostage situations involving political terrorists. Officers at the lower ranks feel that the kinds of operational questions they would inquire about are not covered in the exchanges of policy and policy-related concerns that take place among senior officials who more commonly have the opportunity to exchange information.

As my research focused on the hostage negotiation aspect of terrorism, it could not avoid dealing with questions of victimization. Consequently, one of the chapters focuses on the problems of victims and is an outgrowth of interviews conducted with victims as well as knowledge obtained from other individuals who have worked in this area, especially Dr. Frank Ochberg of the National Institute of Mental Health. I was fortunate to obtain another perspective on victimization from Drs. James Titchener and Jacob Lindy at the University of Cincinnati's College of Medicine, Department of Psychiatry, who worked with the survivors of the flood at Buffalo Creek, West Virginia, and the fire at the Beverly Hills, Kentucky Supper Club. I should especially like to thank Dr. Paula Biren for many hours of thought-provoking discussions on the topic of victimization, which included her work with the Buffalo Creek victims as well as her own personal reflections as a survivor of the Holocaust. In the final analysis my observations on victims are my own. I have let stand without further interpretation the observation that some hostage victims did <u>not</u> experience long-term psychological problems <u>from</u> their experiences, although a considerable body of opinion would argue that not only are victims least able to judge the ramifications of their experiences but if trained observers have not been able to find them,it is because they have not looked. The controversy over the existence or nonexistence of long-term effects of victimization has embraced minds more knowledgeable than my own and,I have chosen to let victims speak for themselves on this issue, although I am mindful that depictions of lack of psychological stress may well be far removed from what is really transpiring.

In conducting this research I found that access to victims and even good access to law enforcement personnel and policy makers was not always easy to

obtain. Victims, by the time I was able to contact
them, had already been overly exposed to a variety
of interviews, ranging from the press to law enforcement personnel. In some cases litigation ensued from hostage situations and potential respondents were concerned about jeopardizing their cases.
Other cases were fraught with a concern for the
maintenance of privacy. Victims were best interviewed immediately after the episode,and if later
interviews were to be conducted,they were perhaps
best conducted in circumstances where the victims
could benefit from the experience, as in the interviews conducted by George Washington University for
the victims of the Hanafi Muslim episode or those
conducted by the Department of Psychiatry, University of Cincinnati, for the victims of the Beverly
Hills, Kentucky catastrophe. Otherwise the inter-
viewer is often an intruder, dealing with a reluctant subject, and the quality of information is at
best questionable.

Hostage situations are often controversial.
They can involve and have involved jurisdictional
disputes between agencies, criticism of operations
within agencies by different branches of the same
agency, and praise or criticism from a wide variety
of sources. Law enforcement personnel and policy
makers are generally in the public eye. They are
expert witnesses who know what to say and how to
guard against what would have the appearance of
controversy. I found that some individuals out-
rightly refused to talk to me about anything remotely controversial. On some occasions one source
provided information totally at variance with that
obtained from another source, and only after second
interviews with the initial source or interviews
with other sources could I gain any degree of confidence in what I felt I could say. On one occasion, after tape recording an interview with an
official for over an hour, he turned to me and
said, "If you turn that thing off, I'll tell you
what really happened." What transpired in the
course of the next hour had little to do with what
went before.

Part of getting information was building access,
"networking" as they call it in Washington. The
experience of obtaining information in this fashion,
through access, with references, and then looking
at the quality of some of it, especially on the
first round, led me to question the entire more
common enterprise of going from randomly selected
policy maker to policy maker with questionnaire in

hand. For if obtaining information with references
presented limitations and difficulties, how much
more limited was the information obtained when unknown interviewers presenting themselves with fixed
questionnaires before policy makers?

I mentioned these caveats because they are necessary in interpreting the conclusions presented.
These conclusions are not etched in granite, but interpretations from interviews that occurred in a
variety of different contexts with a variety of different degrees of openness. Readers, especially
those with first-hand knowledge of the matters discussed in this book, will have to interpret my information in terms of their own experiences. I am
reminded that research involves doing the best one
can with the means at one's disposal.

As the study of contemporary terrorism is relatively new to academia, it has largely consisted of
descriptive work. There have been few attempts at
systematic empirical work and little in the way of
theoretical incision or the generation of theory.
This is to be expected of any new field of inquiry.
It is not, however, the status of the field alone
which accounts for that. Obtaining information on
actual, as opposed to publicly revealed, government
policy on the handling of terrorist episodes or the
manner in which law enforcement agents dealt with
an actual terrorist situation is quite a different
undertaking from obtaining information on policy in
such less sensitive areas as health care, the environment, or education.

Having been at least in close proximity to the
corridors of decision making and having carried
government credentials, I have had more than one
occasion to ponder the utility or research far removed from the focal point of decision making and
from the relatively private, as opposed to the public, thoughts of decision makers. One such experience occurred at a recent academic meeting, when an
able scholar presented a well-researched paper on
government policy on terrorism. There was one major
flaw with the paper: it came exclusively from publicly disseminated sources. The researcher's conclusions were not inappropriate given his data, but
they had little to do with the actual undertakings
of government policy. Before any meaningful the-
orizing or even systematic empirical work can take
place, it is imperative that there be available an
accumulation of reliable, descriptive information.
The acquisition of such information will not come
from public documents alone. In fact, as it is

commonly known in dealing with sensitive issues, it is not uncommon for memoranda to be created for the files, or even to be sent through channels, which everyone knows to be false. One hopes that such documents will not later become the basis for a scholarly work on policy making. The utility of accurate descriptive information is not readily appreciated in academic circles. It would be if academicians were more knowledgeable of the difficulties involved in obtaining such information. Undoubtedly, the generation of systematic empirical and theoretical work would be highly valuable to the conduct of inquiry in this area. When it does emerge, hopefully it will be based on reliable descriptive information.

It is also hoped that systematic and theoretically relevant research will not come to mean, as it has in so many substantive areas of the social sciences, the translation of the obvious into jargon. After all, the full role of the academician in this area will not come about by communicating only with other academicians but by providing observations that will also be relevant to policy makers and operations personnel.

A number of people in various positions in federal and local government and in foreign governments assisted me in this project. They remain anonymous. This is not a measure of ingratitude but a means of preserving the confidentiality with which I have been entrusted.

I should also like to thank Yonah Alexander and Robert Friedlander, fellow scholars in terrorism, who provided a sounding board for a number of the ideas in this project. My co-fellows at LEAA, Gerald Caiden, Robert Gaensslen, and Paul Wice, shared in my intellectual and emotional struggle with this undertaking. I should like to thank them for their contributions to the mutual aid society we created that helped one another persevere when doors were closed and various kinds of access became difficult, if not at times non-existent. Gerald Caplan and Jeffery Alprin, of LEAA, helped open some of those doors, as did my co-fellow Joan Jaccoby, Roberta Lesh, of the Police Foundation, and Lt. Colonel Everett Mann, U.S. Army, retired. I thank them.

Sharon Koehler typed the manuscript with a special sense of attention and concern, and Kate Browne diligently assisted in the creation of the Index.

Abraham H. Miller
Cincinnati, Ohio

REFERENCES

1. Abraham H. Miller, Louis H. Bolce, and Mark R. Halligan, "The New Urban Blacks," <u>Ethnicity</u>, 3 (December 1976),pp. 338-367.

2. Abraham H. Miller, "Peoples Park: Dimensions of a Campus Confrontation," <u>Politics and Society</u>, 2 (Summer, 1972), pp. 433-45.

James McEvoy and Abraham H. Miller, "On Strike Shut It Down...The Crisis at San Francisco State College," <u>Trans-action</u>, 6 (March 1969).

3. Abraham H. Miller, Louis H. Bolce, and Mark R. Halligan, "The J-Curve Theory and the Black Urban Riots," <u>The American Political Science Review</u>, LXXI (September 1977), pp. 964-982.

Terrorism and Hostage Negotiations

1
Introduction: International Terrorism, a Type of Warfare

International terrorism as a type of warfare (as distinct from a tactic within a type of warfare) grew out of the failure of some national liberation movements to achieve results and their inability to develop sufficient political strength to make guerrilla warfare or a full-scale mass movement possible. Because of this political impotency, terrorists seek to attack symbolic enemies. It is generally argued that attacks by national liberation movements against uninvolved Western powers occur because terrorists see their plight as being created by omnipresent capitalist exploiters; however, this is generally a rationale to expand the scope of activity to "soft" targets and thereby assuage the terrorists' feelings of impotentcy. It is worth noting in this regard that Middle-Eastern spawned terrorism sprang up after the 1967 War, a war in which the Israelis devastated guerrilla bases and also exploded the myth that a Palestinian state would be brought about as a result of a military victory achieved by sympathetic and powerful Arab states. When the Palestinians, in response, changed their tactics from guerrilla warfare to terrorism, the targets were not within Israel but in the skies flown by aircraft of security casual Western nations.

In the face of overwhelming defeat, or in the face of weakness, how does a national liberation movement preserve its momentum and prevent the faithful from retiring to apathy? This is the problem which terrorist groups and all politically weak

1

groups face. The solution is sometimes found in the
substitution of symbolic victories and international
publicity for the unobtainable victories that lead
to real political power.

Terrorism can be seen from two perspectives: (1)
a struggle for liberation from colonial domination,
or perceived domination, and (2) the struggle a-
gainst an allegedly oppressive domestic regime. In
both cases, terrorism occurs because more potent and
meaningful forms of political violence have become
ineffectual or are beyond the resources of the
regimes' opponents. In both cases, access to the
media is an important ingredient. In the struggle
against colonial domination, access to the media is
required to convey a sense of fear and futility to
the overseas capital of colonial power, as well as
in the colony. The message of the terrorist media
campaign is to portray the struggle as costly and
futile. Wars against colonial masters are as likely
to be won by turning around public opinion in the
dominating state as on the battlefield.

Where the struggle is against domestic regimes,
the use of the media is tied to the philosophical
rationale based on a rather vulgar interpretation
of Marx's assertion that revolutions come about because of the increasing misery of the exploited
masses. The terrorists' translation of Marx's
notion is that an oppressive regime when confronted
with instability and insecurity through political
terrorism will become even more brutal and repres-
sive in attempting to stop terrorism. The increased
oppressiveness of the regime, coupled with its de-
clining legitimacy ensuing from its inability to
preserve order, will, so the terrorists theorize,
create an inevitable popular uprising. The same
philosophical rationale was used in the late 1960's
by the Weather Underground to launch the "days of
rage" in Chicago where sporadic violence was initiated against the business district.

The events of Chicago were to prove what common
sense might have dictated, the terrorists's philosophical rationale was not only bad Marxism but bad
tactics. Common sense, however, was of little concern to the Weather Underground and is apparently
of little concern to most doctrinaire terrorists.
When a committed terrorist perceives himself operating within the framework of historical inevita-
bility, as revealed by Marxist-Leninism, then prag-
matic considerations relating to tactics are often
meaningless.

The philosophical position of Marx and Engels

on terrorism is actually best described as ambiguous. The Marxist doctrine is fundamentally concerned with political change through revolution. Revolutions are mass uprisings that occur in accord with specific social and historical conditions. In contrast, terrorism is generally created through individual acts of violence without the prerequisite mass base required for full-scale revolution. According to Marx, revolutions, not acts of terrorism, are the locomotives of history.

Marx and Engels bitterly parted company with Michael Bakunin and his philosophy of anarchistic terrorism, seeing it as a counterproductive force. However, Marx and Engels were not completely inflexible on their position regarding terrorism. They were able and willing to make allowances for the Russian terrorist movements of the late nineteenth century as reflective of the unique conditions that existed in Russia. Lenin and Trotsky, however, were quite opposed to the indiscriminate use of terrorism even in Russia.

In the contemporary setting, the philosophical position of Marxism has been meaningful only when communist-oriented terrorist groups can find a rationale for their activities in some interpretation of Marxist thought, even if the interpretation is convoluted. Such communist-oriented modern terrorist groups as Baader-Meinhof, the Italian Red Brigade,or the Popular Front for the Liberation of Palestine have, like America's Weather Underground, found philosophical rationales in Marxism for the use of terrorism, and the Soviet KGB has been actively involved in training and funding terrorist movements. Ironically, terrorism has not generally been a threat to authoritarian Communist regimes, where terrorism is a monopoly of the state. It is liberal democracies which are most vulnerable to terrorism, and terrorists exploit the freedoms of liberal democracy to achieve their goals.

TERRORISM AND DEMOCRACY

Freedom of travel, association, speech, and the press, integral components of the liberal democratic state, are all subject to exploitation by terrorists. The migration of workers from one country to another and the ensuing establishment of ethnic enclaves,where terrorists from abroad find Mao's proverbial sea to swim in, is an additional vulnerability of Western democracies. The existence of such communities not only makes the foreign-looking terrorist less obtrusive, but among his fellow countrymen the terrorist might even find a fertile area for sowing the seeds of dissention. Here sympathizers, resources, and new recruits can be found.

The geographical proximity of European democracies to KGB training grounds in Eastern Europe further heightens the vulnerability of these democracies to terrorism. Indeed, one of the speculations about the lack of success of foreign terrorists in the United States has often revolved around its geographical distance from safe havens.

The liberal democracies confronted by active and continuous terrorist operations face difficult choices. The very freedoms liberal democracies value as part of their cherished sense about themselves is what enables terrorists to operate. Where the state controls the monopoly on political terrorism, anti-state terrorism is virtually non-existent, but the creation of an environment which eliminates the freedoms terrorists need to survive also means the creation of an environment which would destroy the liberal democratic state. This is effect would mean doing what the terrorists themselves set out to do but were unable to accomplish. In Uruguay, for example, the Tupamaros, a self-styled Marxist terrorist group, managed to bring about a right-wing reaction against the liberal state. The elimination of basic liberties caused greater oppression of the masses, but with the destruction of the liberal state did not come the popular uprising the Tupamaros anticipated. Instead, the right-wing coup d'etat not only eliminated the liberal state, but with it all political opposition, including the Tupamaros.

It is not, however, necessary for the liberal democracy confronted with terrorism to ignore it and continue its policy process on a "business as usual" footing. It is sometimes assumed Western democracies will have to learn to live with terrorism the way in which American cities have learned to live with street crime and violence. Such sentiments, in a certain sense, are not entirely inappropriate, for they illustrate that while terrorism is an irritant, the larger society continues to function around it. On a statistical basis, the total cost in dollars and lives by terrorism worldwide since 1968, is less that the cost of crime in any mid-sized American city for any one year. Seeing terrorism solely in these terms, however,

ignores some of the more important and less calcu-
lable costs of terrorism. Terrorism, in the short
run, is concerned primarily with the manipulation of
political symbols as a means of getting access to or
controlling the international public agenda. Terrorists design operations which by their very nature are media events, generating for the terrorists
an inordinant amount of publicity. But it is not
simply access to the agenda which terrorists seek,
and too often terrorist activities are seen solely
from that perspective; more important, and often
less considered, is the control which terrorists
seek over the agenda. The assassination of a major
political figure is not only a media event from
which a terrorist group derives much sought-after
publicity, but the death of a significant political
figure can cause major changes in policy and can
even disrupt the world order.

The omnipresent street crime that urban Americans have of necessity learned to live with gnaws
slowly at the legitimacy of the society, but major
terrorist episodes can call into question the legitimacy and effectiveness of a regime to the point
of shaking it to its very roots. It is not useful
to view terrorism from the same exact perspective as
street crime, as a contemporary problem to which
the citizenry must and will acclimate.

Although Western democracies are well advised
not to overract to terrorism, they are equally well
advised not to dismiss it as insignificant. In
fact, despite public pronouncements to the contrary,
terrorism, as viewed by the Carter administration,
is not seen as a serious domestic problem. The
United States has not chosen a posture of leadership
among Western democracies in their conflict with
international terrorism.

If the government does not take terrorism as
seriously as it should, the media has rushed to over
compensate by taking terrorism too seriously. The
media thrives on poignant drama, and the visual
media thrives on spectacle. Terrorism, as we have
come to know it, is to some extent the creation of
the media. The media is the unwitting accomplice of
terrorism and not without some lack of options at
times in terms of its participation. After all, the
media's job is to report the news, and the actions
of a terrorist group are generally newsworthy. As
we are all too aware, terrorism is theatre, and
much of it is undertaken solely for dramatic effect.
This does not put the drama outside the concern of
the media. It does, however, suggest some concern

about how the drama is reported. Recently, the major television networks and members of the newspaper media have acknowledged that greater responsibility is necessary, both in the media's depiction of terrorists and the manner in which the media have attempted to obtain information at the scene of terrorist incidents. Too often, the media have interfered with the police operation and released information which assisted the terrorists.

Overzealous reporters have hampered police operations, unwittingly served as the eyes and ears of terrorists, and have released information which threatened the lives of innocent victims. A number of examples are given in the course of this work. However, one of the most poignant examples comes from Thomas M. Ashwood, Chairman of Flight Security for the International Pilots Association. As Ashwood notes, "Yesterday I spent an entire day with the head of the German pilot's association.... I am convinced that the media was involved in that hijacking over there [referring to the hijacking of an October 1977 Lufthansa flight by terrorists which was brought to an end by the daring West German raid at Mogadishu] and was to a large degree responsible for the death of the captain. The fact is that the ongoing reporting over the radio--the public radio-- the fact that it was announced over the radio that the captain was passing information very cleverly with his normal radio transmission was heard by the terrorist on board the aircraft, and I believe this was a major factor leading to the captain's execution."[1]

For the liberal democratic state, the problems raised by the intrusion of the media into anti- terrorist operations are inordinately complex. In the United States, these problems revolve around the conflict between safeguarding lives and preserving first amendment freedoms. The tension between these two values, at least in the context of anti- terrorist operations, may ultimately find its way to the courts for resolution. The news media have consistently maintained that they must be at the scene of an event in order to report the news. To some extent, this right has been upheld in the courts to the point where many urban police departments incorporate procedures which permit the press this kind of access.

The right to gather news, however, like freedom of the press, is not an absolute right. In <u>Houchins v. KQED, Inc.</u>, Chief Justice Burger stated the <u>United States</u> Supreme Court's view that one cannot infer that the right to speak and publish carries with it the unrestrained right to gather information.[2]

In dealing with political terrorism, a democratic society must often choose between the maintenance of order and security on the one hand and freedom on the other. As Paul Wilkinson has noted, "...no liberal democrat is willing to pay the price of human freedom simply in order to achieve total political obedience or submission. To believe that it is worth snuffing out all individual rights and sacrificing liberal values for the sake of order is to fall into the error of the terrorists themselves, the folly of believing the end justifies the means."[3] Wilkinson goes on to note that the attempts to abandon the structural foundation of liberal democracy when dealing with internal terrorism become tempting and must be resisted. Yet, liberal democracy, as Wilkinson further notes, must avoid the failure to uphold constitutional authority and the rule of law. Wilkinson's solution to the two-horned dilemma is to have strong security which is subjected to the democratic process within the law.

Civil libertarians, however, will respond to Wilkinson's approach by asking, "What is the rule of law?" Certainly, it is possible for a government to function within the rule of law, but what will be the content of those laws? Reasonable men will differ on the cost to society of the different emphases which the law can render. Some will emphasize freedom at the price of security and others will propose the opposite. The law, moreover, is not carved in granite but subject to the interpretation of jurists, who reflect not only their own private values but in a democracy realize the necessity of considering public values. Consequently, the rule of law can, even within the basic ethos of liberal democracy, produce dramatically different results. Former FBI Director Clarence Kelly has argued, "If we are to have any degree of success in solving the cases now confronting us in terrorism... we must have all the tools available to us, including electronic surveillance."[4] And former Canadian Prime Minister Pierre Elliott Trudeau, responding to the terrorist campaign in Quebec in 1970, noted, "When terrorists and urban guerrillas were trying to provoke the secession of Quebec, I made it clear that I wouldn't hesitate to send in the army and I did, despite the anguished cries of civil libertarians."[5] Similarly, legal scholar Robert Friedlander

has argued, "If the state truly wishes to protect
itself from the threat and destruction of terror
violence, then social order must be strengthened at
the expense of individual freedom."[6] Those are
rather strong statements, and it is highly doubtful
that they would find unequivocal support among the
public at large. The answer to the dilemma posed
by a democratic society's need for freedom and security, however, will not be found in the context
of abstract issues, but more than likely will e-
merge through the challenge of responding to actual
terrorist events.

TERRORISM AND THE UNITED NATIONS

One arena where the challenge of the ongoing
assault of terrorists on society has not been faced
is within the United Nations. Nowhere is the
cliche, "One man's terrorist is another man's freedom fighter," more in evidence than in the heated
but largely unproductive debates over terrorism
within the UN. The different value orientations
which terrorism evokes has hampered effective action
by the UN in this domain. In September 1972, the
United States put forth a proposal which sought to
establish several typical terrorist-type operations
as punishable offenses and to be dealt with through
the remedy of extradite or prosecute. The United
States sponsored resolution did not pass.

In December 1972, the United Nations did adopt
a resolution on international terrorism. Unfortunately, it sounded more like a justification for
terrorism than a condemnation. The document portrayed terrorism as emanating from, "misery, frus-
tration, grievance and despair...which cause some
people to sacrifice human lives, including their
own, in an attempt to effect radical social
change."[7] The only type of terrorism which the
resolution acknowledged was that of so-called "colonial" and "racist" regimes denying people their
right to self-determination. The implication of the
document is that the former type of terrorism is
justified, and the UN is incapable of showing any
compassion for the indiscriminate taking of innocent
human life as long as the motivation for such
killings is to bring about radical social change.
Interestingly, the resolution also ignores state
terrorism of the type so widely practiced among the
majority of autocratic governments which dominate
the UN.

A realistic response to the problem, or any great moral condemnation of terrorism,cannot be expected from this body. Terrorists are often clients of UN member states which have used terrorism as an extension of diplomacy. This fact was dramatically illustrated when Benin, the Libyan Arab Republic, and Tanzania entered a resolution before the security council to condemn Israel for the daring rescue of its nationals at Entebbe. The resolution completely disregarded Article 51 of the United Nations Charter which permits "the inherent right of individual or collective self-defense," and serves as the juridical basis for the norm of forcible self-help and the historic remedy of humanitarian intervention.[8]

Although the United Nations has been unable to pass a resolution protecting innocent men, women and children from indiscriminate murder, being duly concerned with the increased incidents of terrorism against diplomats and public officials, the UN, through General Assembly Resolution 3166, made murder, kidnaping, or other attacks upon the person or liberty of a designated "internationally protected person" an offense punishable by all member states which are signatories to the convention. The resolution goes on to note, "The State Party in whose territory one alleged offender is present is obliged if it does not extradite him, submit, without exception whatsoever and without undue delay, the case to its competent authorities for the purpose of prosecution...." Contracting authorities are further permitted to consider the convention as the legal basis for extradition.[9]

The glaring contrast between the UN's ability to protect diplomats and its inability to protect innocents has not been lost on policy makers and the mass public in Western democracies; nor has been the fact that certain UN members, among them Libya, Syria, North Korea, and the Soviet Union, most notably, have been sponsors, recruiters, and directors of terrorist organizations and their operations. These nations have compromised the UN's role in this area. Western democracies have also found it impossible to rely on Interpol because any state which is part of the Interpol network, including those which sponsor terrorist organizations, can gain access to Interpol files and information.

International cooperation is consequently limited to exchanges of technology, information, and mutual assistance between Western nations; however, as previously noted, Eastern block countries have cooperated in apprehending terrorists, as in the case of responding to extradition requests from West Germany. The inconsistency in behavior of the Eastern block might have resulted from a need to obtain legitimacy for its public disavowal of terrorist activities, while clandestinely supporting certain terrorist groups and operations.

Generally speaking, the reaction of Eastern block nations to the issues raised on the international agenda by terrorism have tended to be a function of how they perceive their own vulnerability to terrorism. For example, the Soviet Union continually sided with the Arab States in their attempts to block UN General Assembly resolutions dealing with hijacking, and until October 1970, the Soviet propaganda apparatus justified the behavior of Arab terrorists. The Soviet position was radically changed with the experience of the Soviet vulnerability to terrorists. In October 1970, two Lithuanians hijacked a Soviet domestic airliner, killing a stewardess and wounding the pilot and copilot. The Lithuanians flew to Turkey where they received diplomatic asylum. Prompted by this experience to change dramatically their policy, the Soviet Union, despite Arab opposition, supported the UN General Assembly resolution of November 25, 1970 condemning hijacking.

The support of the anti-hijacking resolution did not change the Soviet position toward the PLO, but, as a result of the October 1970 incident, the Soviets appeared better to understand the consequence of having heavily armed dissidents wreaking havoc with the international network of air transportation and realized that the Soviet airlines were not immune to such attacks.

TERRORISM: THE OPERATION OF CONTEXT

Clearly, the Soviet response to terrorism--like that of many other nations--is a case of whose ox has been or is about to be gored. For this reason, the concept of "terrorism" when discussed in the international policy domain escapes definition. It is not that "terrorism" is intrinsically more difficult to define than any other political concept, but "terrorism" escapes definition when it becomes embellished with value-ladened, political meaning.

From my perspective, terrorism is first and foremost an act of political violence. It is not a tactic but a strategic mode of political violence.

It is generally, but not exclusively, directed at targets which have symbolic value in addition to or independent of any tactical or strategic value. It is the symbolic value which usually transcends the direct significance of any specific target, and is aimed at influencing political decision making through fear and intimidation. One of the primary ingredients of political terrorism is random violence. Where all people are targets and no one is safe, fear is heightened because it is difficult to escape into safety wrought by noninvolvement in the ongoing political struggle. Political terrorism can be and often is used by those in power as well as by those attempting to attain power; however, I would prefer to think of the term "political terrorism" as a means of defining the behavior of non-state actors and the term "state terrorism" as a means of defining the actions of state actors.

In law enforcement circles within the United States, "terrorism" has come to be identified with a criminal mode of operation rather than with the specific intent or motivation of the actors. Such acts as bombings, kidnappings, hostage and barricade situations, and assassinations are generally spoken of as terrorist activities. The issue is only whether victims have been terrorized and the law has been broken. Any other considerations become unimportant, because tactically the law enforcement response is going to be the same. The basic question which law enforcement agents ask is whether or not the tactics they use in what they call terrorist situations will work against political terrorists, who are viewed to be organized, prepared, and dedicated.

Although political terrorism does not appear to be taken seriously within much of the federal bureaucracy, local law enforcement is very concerned with this subject. Local law enforcement has been in the forefront of the efforts to devise tactics to deal with some of the more familiar types of terrorist operations. From the perspective of local law enforcement, they, and not the federal government, will be in the front lines when (and not if) political terrorism strikes hard on the domestic scene. Most local law enforcement officials feel it is only a matter of time when this happens, and in the meantime the repertoire of their skills increases as their techniques are used against operations committed by felons.

This book is about one of those types of terrorist operations where local law enforcement through

experience has developed considerable expertise.
The work deals with the techniques used in hostage
and barricade situations, episodes where hostages
are taken, a barricade situation ensues, and demands
are made on the authorities for the hostages' release. By using a mixture of disciplined force and
psychological manipulation, law enforcement agents
have been very successful in bringing about the capitulation of terrorists in a variety of different
hostage and barricade circumstances.

The focus of this work is directed at the actual
application of hostage and barricade methods in circumstances varying from confrontation with felons
on the domestic scene to confrontations both here
and abroad with political terrorists. In order to
understand these methods, it is necessary to view
them against a series of significantly related issues which affect these types of operations. Consequently, it is necessary to discuss terrorism in
terms of its general attributes: its need to create
spectacular drama and influence the media; its use
of violence to intimidate society beyond the impact
on individual victims; and the policy-oriented response of our government to the spectre of violence
created by political terrorists.

Through consideration of the aforementioned
issues, from analyses of specific cases involving
hostage and barricade situations, and through discussions of the methods and operations used by law
enforcement agents here and abroad, it is hoped
that a better understanding of modern terrorism and
the ability of liberal democracies to cope with its
methods will be rendered.

REFERENCES

1. Thomas M. Ashwood, remarks to the "Terrorism and the Media" Conference held at the City University of New York, November 17, 1977.
2. For an in-depth discussion of this issue,
see: Juanita Jones and Abraham H. Miller, "Terrorism and the Media: Resolving the First Amendment
Dilemma," Ohio Northern University Law Review,
forthcoming.
3. Paul Wilkinson, Terrorism and the Liberal
State (London: The Macmillam Press, Ltd., 1977),
p. 122.
4. Quoted in Robert A. Friedlander, ed., Terrorism: Documents of International and Local Control
(Dobbs Ferry, New York: Oceana Publications, Inc.,

1979), p. 112.

5. Ibid., p. 113.

6. Ibid., p. 114.

7. "Resolution Adopted by the United Nations General Assembly," Twenty-seventh Session [A/8969, A/L.696], December 1972.

8. For an excellent discussion of this issue, see: Robert A. Friedlander, op. cit., pp. 89-92.

9. "Resolution Adopted by the United Nations General Assembly," Twenty-eight Session, [A/Res 3166 (XXVIII)], February 5, 1974.

2
Negotiations for Hostages: Implications from the Police Experience

INTRODUCTION: THE CASE OF THE HANAFI MUSLIMS

On Thursday, March 10, 1977, in Washington, D.C., a small group of members of an otherwise inconspicuous black sect of Muslims precipitated the first hostage situation in the United States executed by ideologically motivated and organized terrorists. Armed with guns and machetes, the band of Hanafi Muslims seized hostages at the national headquarters of the B'nai B'rith, the Jewish social service agency; the Islamic Center; and the City Council chambers in the District of Columbia Building. The small group of heavily armed men created a drama that spread fear throughout Washington. Security at government buildings was intensified, and protection was provided for City Council members and several congressmen.

As news of the incident, buttressed by live television coverage from the three locations, punctuated the lives of the city's residents, the pall of fear could be felt in the air. A snarl of the city's rush hour traffic, resulting from police blockades at the three locations, was simply one more reminder that the psychological impact of the drama being played out in the city's northwest corridor reached beyond the confinement of the hostages.

The most devastating aspect of terror is its uncertainty. Random violence is a haunting violence, leaving no room for the security of delusion. It is random violence that is such a crucial component of the rise of modern-day totalitarianism and what separates it from other forms of dictatorship. In the nontotalitarian dictatorship, one can at least aspire to be politically neutral, and in so doing perhaps avoid the attention of the

14

secret police. In totalitarian states, there is
no such security, no such delusion of neutrality.
Enemies of the state are not individuals but cat-
egories of people. Individuals are arrested because they are members of a category in a state
where the primary purpose of the political police
is not to apprehend criminals but to define crim-
inality. Individual behavior provides no guaran-
tees against finding oneself in a category that
has been defined as criminal and selected for processing through the penal system. The randomness of
the draw creates the climate of fear and uncertainty that provides for the unstable environment in
which totalitarianism flourishes.

The late and brilliant political scientist
Hannah Arendt[1] painstakingly and insightfully described the role of random terror in the creation
of the totalitarian state as a sui generis political institution. However, the functions of random terror are not only available and amenable to
those who hold and seek to perpetuate power but
also to whose who wish to seize it. If random terror can promote the social and political instability that will create an environment conducive to
the maintenance of charismatic leadership, the
smae instrument unleashed against a stable society
can promote an environment conductive to repression,
instability, and the loss of a government's legitimacy. Random violence promotes fear. Stable
governments, let alone stable democracies, have
never thrived in an environment of fear.

It is this ingredient of randomness, this sense
of fear wrought by uncertainty, that made the psychological impact of the Hanafi seizures so terrifying. There was nothing predictable in the events
that led from the brutal slayings, four years earlier, of seven members of the Hanafi community, to
the shotgun blast that killed twenty-four-year-old
Maurice Williams, a reporter for Washington's WHUR-
FM. Williams, a black Howard University graduate,
had only recently been assigned to the District
government beat. His death, like the wounding and
beating of other innocents, could only be properly
understood as the result of his being at the wrong
place at the wrong time--a contingency against which
neutrality is no prophylaxis. To learn of Williams's ironic death was to project one's own
vulnerability. In that comprehension the most
devastating aspect of terrorism is revealed.

Although twelve men were indicted for their
actions in the episode, informed and knowledgeable

observers see the drama as having been written by
one man, Hamass Abdul Khaalis, age fifty-four.
Khaalis has been described as an articulate, dramatic man with a history of mental illness. It
was Khaalis's ability as a charismatic leader that
made the operation possible. Observers commented
that many of the others neither fully knew nor
completely understood the consequences of what
they were doing.

During the past four years, Khaalis had been
burdened by the brutal murders of the seven members of his community. Four of the victims were
children, including a nine-day-old baby. They
were drowned in a sink. Two women and another
child had been shot from close range. A former
member of the U.S. attorney's office who had seen
the corpses said to me in the aftermath of the recent episode, "If ever a guy had cause for vengeance, this guy [Khaalis[had cause."

The murders had been committed by five Black
Muslims after Khaalis had circulated a letter, in
December of 1972, to fifty-seven temples of the
Nation of Islam. In that letter, he denounced
Elijah Muhammad, the spiritual leader of the Nation
of Islam. It was alleged that the conspiracy behind the murders reached into the Black Muslim
hierarchy, but aside from the seven men originally
indicted, two of whom were subsequently acquitted,
no one else has been charged with the slayings.
This embittered the Hanafis.

The trial of the alleged murders was not perceived as having gone well for the Hanafis. Judge
Leonard Braman acquitted one defendant when an un-
indicted coconspirator refused to testify. Another
defendant was granted a new trial by Braman after
a jury had returned a verdict of guilty. The
second trial resulted in a mistrial when Amina
Khaalis, a survivor of the slaughter and daughter
of the group's leader, refused to submit to cross-
examination. Amina Khaalis still suffers from
bullet fragments in her head.

During the course of the trial, Khaalis had
become agitated, and several times he disrupted
the proceedings. He was fined $750 for this, and
he viewed it with the bitterness of having had
insult added to injury.

Judge Braman's handling of the case was seen,
by Khaalis, as further confirmation of a Jewish
conspiracy that ultimately controlled the Black
Muslims. Braman is Jewish. Ironically, the Black
Muslim defendants asked Braman to withdraw from the

case because of this religion. The five men who were convicted each received sentences of over one hundred and forty years.

Khaalis's disappointment at the trial was underscored by a recent political loss when the established Arab governments recognized Wallace Muhammad, Elijah Muhammad's successor, as the trustee and spokesman for all American Muslim organizations. It was this recognition that is seen as having provided not only the motivation for the seizure of the Islamic Center and the involvement of representatives of the international Islamic community in the hostage episode, but also the primary motivation behind the seizures, perhaps even beyond the concern for vengeance.

It was from elements that grew out of the slaughter, the ensuing judicial proceedings, and finally the intervention of Arab governments on behalf of the Nation of Islam that the Hanafis's choice of targets was determined. The B'nai B'rith was chosen because of the perception of Jewish control of the Black Muslims; the Islamic Center because of the involvement of the international Islamic community in supporting the Black Muslims; and the District government because of the perceived failure of the government to provide justice. Thus, the first political hostage situation in the United State emerged.

HOSTAGE NEGOTIATION POLICY: FOREIGN AND DOMESTIC

In the course of my interviews with hostage negotiators and tactical units in our urban police, it became overwhelmingly evident that the police have believed that a political hostage situation was imminent. In fact, in face of the rise of terrorism, it was considered an accident of good fortune that no politically motivated hostage situation had previously occurred. Not that the police had been unprepared for such encounters, but the strategy and tactics of police operations in dealing with hostage negotiations had never before been implemented where the captors had been ideologically organized and motivated. No one knew whether in the face of ideologically motivated terrorists the carefully orchestrated procedures of police negotiation techniques would work. No one really wanted to find out.

Since the tragedy of the 1972 Munich Olympics,

the American police have been developing tactics to
deal with terrorist-hostage situations. Some of
the most able and best known work has grown out of
a hostage negotiation school developed by psychol-
ogist Harvey Schlossberg and detective Captain
Frank Bolz, both of the New York Police Department.
Underwritten by the Law Enforcement Assistance Administration, the school has trained police from
other municipalities and from foreign countries in
the psychological drama of negotiating for hostages.
Similar training is given to domestic police through
the Federal Bureau of Investigation Academy at
Quantico, Virginia.

Although the details of the training are beyond
the concerns of this chapter, domestic training
places are a premium on securing the safe release
of hostages, often at the expense of some bartering
with the captors. In every police department there
are parameters with regard to bargaining, but bargaining, giving and getting something in return, is
the primary mode of hostage negotiation as carried
on by the domestic police. The success rate of
this policy has been incredible. In New York City,
in over four hundred situations, the safety of both
victim and captor has been secured without death or
injury. And similar success rates can be found in
other municipalities.

For all ostensible purposes, domestic policy
appears to run directly counter to the official
policy of the United States government, which re-
fuses to enter into negotiations for the release of
hostages. This policy has been publicly enunci-
ated by former Secretary of State Henry Kissinger[2]
and reiterated by Ambassador Douglas Heck,[3] special
assistant to the secretary of state and coordinator
for combating terrorism.

The official posture and the publicly espoused
message is that the United States government has
not and will not pay ransom, release prisoners, or
otherwise yield to terrorist demands. Moreover,
the government will not negotiate such issues. On
the other hand, the government will conduct discussions with terrorists to secure the release of
hostages. As one State Department member said to
me in an attempt to clarify this elliptic policy,
"We will talk but we will not negotiate." Negotiation in this context means a bartering of hostages for tangible demands, while talking means an
inquiry into the well-being of the hostages and
appeals on humanitarian grounds for their release.

In defense of this policy Henry Kissinger has noted that the problem of hostage negotiation, at least from the perspective of the government, must be viewed in the context of thousands of Americans who are in jeopardy all over the world. From this perspective, acquiescence to terrorist demands is seen as a stimulus to increased and continuing terror against Americans across the globe.[4]

The supposition here is that the public declaration that the government will not negotiate acts as a deterrent against terrorist attack. The empirical foundations for this supposition, however, have not been demonstrated.

The Israelis maintain a similar policy. One highly placed Israeli official informed me that they are convinced their policy works and that the number of terrorist episodes is reduced because of it. He argues that material from interrogation of captured terrorists indicates that the policy of nonnegotiation, sometimes referred to as "surrender or die," makes recruitment very difficult for terrorist missions inside Israel.

As we will note later, there is some question as to just how effective the policy of nonnegotiation is, despite what some officials might think. Admittedly, the hostage takers that domestic police encounter have not been political terrorists. But they are often very desperate people and one wonders to what extent the overwhelming success rate of our domestic police can be facilely dismissed by simply saying that they are not dealing with political terrorists. It is this statement that makes the Hanafi case so interesting. Not only were the Hanafis politically motivated and organized, but the political motivation was underscored with personal vengeance.

THE TACTICAL RESPONSE OF THE POLICE

The Hanafi leader made three demands on the authorities: (1) the cessation of a movie starring Anthony Quinn and titled, Muhammad: Messenger of God, which the Hanafis found offensive; (2) the return to Khaalis of the $750 fine imposed by Judge Braman; and (3) the handing over to Khaalis the five Black Muslims who had been convicted of the massacre at the Hanafi house.

Police prepared for the long wait, which is the primary tactic in situations such as this, which call for giving the drama time to unfold. Special

police weapons teams set up a controlled inner
perimeter. Fire power and tactical support from
sharpshooters and shotgun-carrying police were imposed on the inner perimeter. An external perimeter that cordoned off the sites and diverted traffic was maintained by regular police. A phone link
was established at all three sites with the gunmen.
It was procedure by the book, the kind used in every hostage situation. But this event was unique.

Its uniqueness resided in the motivations and
demands of the gunmen. They had wanted to take
hostages. The locations were chosen for political
and symbolic reasons. The motivation was reinforced by an underlying ideological commitment.
Intelligence information revealed that they had
mentally and physically prepared for a long siege.
A killing and a shoot-out with police had already
taken place at the District Building. The captors
had no apparent hope of obtaining sanctuary on foreign soil. It seemed to be a classic political
terrorist operation, and the structural aspects
appeared to stand as testimony to the gunmen's
determination.

While it is true that the police are experienced
in dealing with desperate people, it is also true
that few of the hostage takers they encounter are
willing to die for their demands. Most hostage
takers willing to die are suicidal types who want
the police to do to them what they are unable to
do themselves. But generally these individuals are
not interested in slaying their captives.

The most common hostage experience that the police encounter is with the professional felon who
in the course of committing a crime finds himself
interrupted and without escape. He seizes hostages.
Initially that looks as if it will provide a way
out. Ultimately, it becomes a liability, and the
professional felon is rational enough to recognize
just what a liability it is. Armed robbery is an
easier sentence to face than is murder or kidnapping. The felon is willing to cut his losses.
Some police feel that the successful outcome of such
episodes, with due respect to the elaborate psychological theories sustaining hostage negotiation
techniques, is because the felon neither wants to
die nor face a murder charge. One experienced police negotiator noted that in the final analysis,
when dealing with an interrupted felon holding
hostage, the job of the negotiator is to convince
the perpetrator that if he surrenders, the awesome
display of flack-jacketed and heavily armed police

who are confronting him will be restrained.

What has troubled most police about the encounter with the political terrorist is the perception by police that terrorists are willing to die and die dramatically if their demands are not met. In my interviews with negotiators and special weapons personnel around the country, I have found this to be the overwhelming concern when police talk about applying hostage negotiation techniques to a drama involving political terrorists.

Although, such perceptions are widely held, they are terribly inaccurate. According to data generated from the Central Intelligence Agency's Project ITERATE,[5] only 1.2 percent of all transnational terrorist missions undertaken between 1968 and mid-1974 could be categorized as suicidal. Another 35.4 percent of all missions depicted the terrorists as possessing a willingness to die but a preference not to, and 62.8 percent of terrorist missions had elaborate escape plans built into them.

Before the Hanafi incident it was obvious to the police that the tactics and procedures that had generally been used in hostage situations would of necessity be used if the perpetrators were political terrorists. The gnawing question was: Would these procedures be successful? Inferences from one example-albeit the only one--are questionable, but the important and widely overlooked consideration is that political terrorist situations are not as dissimilar from other kinds of hostage situations as we might be predisposed to think, especially after we factor out our stereotypic notions of the suicidal instincts of terrorists. In addition to what the Project ITERATE data tells us about the lack of suicidal predispositions on the part of terrorists, a former highly placed Israeli police official tells me that he can recall only two cases in which terrorists appeared to have committed suicide; and even in these two incidents there was some question as to whether or not they were killed by explosives that might have been set off in an exchange of gunfire rather than by the terrorists.

Irrespective of these considerations, in the Hanafi situation, the police were limited in the options they could exercise. For all practical purposes, the only realistic option was what they had been trained to do and had done in the past, i.e., institute the process of negotiation; establish contact and trust with the gunmen; barter for

things that could be exchanged; and let time play
its crucial role.

Waiting out the subjects is based on the knowledge that as time progresses, there is generally
an intimacy that builds up between the subjects
and the hostages that decreases the likelihood that
the hostages will be killed. This, however, need
not be the case in every situation for if the hostages are dehumanized or initially perceived as
being something less than human the prophylactic
intimacy will not occur. Given the rabid anti-
Semitism of the Hanafi Muslims, it was doubtful if
this aspect of the long wait (at least the B'nai
B'rith location) would result. However, there is
another important element that results from this
tactic. As the situation progresses, the initial
enthusiasm of the perpetrators deteriorates and the
constant prospect of death begins to gnaw at the
captors. The captors too are confined and threatened with violence. And the sight of heavily armed
police in flack jackets and helmets, deployed in
military formation, is a terrifying sight remind-
ing one of one's own mortality and vulnerablity.
The captors begin to realize that they too are captives, albeit of their own making.

In the course of negotiations, the police produced two of the Hanafis's demands. The offending
movie was stopped, and Khaalis's fine was returned.
The Black Muslim killers held in federal prison,
however, were not surrendered. Yet, some things
had been produced. Khaalis certainly could point
to some successes from the episode and save face.[6]

As several of the hostages at the Islamic Center were foreign Moslems and Khaalis requested to
speak to representatives of the international Mos-
lem community, the State Department made arrangements for the ambassadors of Egypt, Iran, and Pa-
kistan to assist with the negotiations. After establishing rapport via phone communication with
Khaalis, the three ambassadors, along with District
of Columbis Police Chief Maurice J. Cullinane and
Deputy Chief Robert L. Rabe, met face to face with
Khaalis. The assembled group sat down at a folding table in a corridor on the first floor of the
B'nai B'rith Building. The ambassadors read to
Khaalis from the Koran about love and compassion.
After the meeting ended without formal or verbal
decision, Iranian Ambassador Ardeshir Zahedi embraced Khaalis in the Middle Eastern manner of saying good-bye. Sometime thereafter, in phone conversations with Cullinane and Rabe, Khaalis agreed

to surrender holding out for one more demand--to
be released on his own recognizance pending trial.
When this demand was approved by a District judge,
the ordeal ended.   After a grueling thirty-eight
hours, the hostages were released.

THE MOTIVATION FOR CAPITULATION: IMPLICATIONS FOR
NEGOTIATION

Why did Khaalis capitulate?   Did the ambassadors persuade him to surrender?   According to
Khaalis's son-in-law, Abdul Aziz, the meeting only
reinforced a decision already made.   Those of us
who have studied hostage situations would argue
that in the end Khaalis realized he too was a hostage and the continuing confrontation with death
was no longer as desirable as it appeared initially.   Beyond that, there are some other considerations.   Aside from the demand for vengeance that
went unfulfilled (and despite its prominence in
the press accounts, it was not a repeated demand,
a factor that led police not to pursue it in the
negotiations, especially since Khaalis himself was
not pursuing it), and despite the subsidiary demands that were fulfilled, something else was a-
chieved.   The larger society had yielded to Khaalis
an otherwise unobtainable amount of publicity for
his cause and for his grievances.   The wisdom of
some of it was questionable, but it was undeniably
massive.   From continuous live television coverage,
to domination of virtually the entire first section
of the Washington Post for two days to trans-At-
lantic phone interviews, the Hanafis were transformed from a little-known group to the focal point
of national and international media coverage.
In these very real and very critical ways, the
Hanafis, like terrorists generally, obtained concessions from the larger society, and that in itself is the primary purpose of much terrorist activity.   According to Project ITERATE data, 37.3
percent of all transnational terrorist activity is
undertaken to obtain specific concessions from the
larger society, the most common set of purposes
attributed to terrorist activity.   Among these,
publicity is a widely sought after concession. Professor Baljit Singh[7] has insightfully noted that
the purpose of most acts of terrorism is to have
otherwise ignored concerns placed prominently on
the public agenda.
While the Hanafi activity was similar in moti-

vation to that of other terrorist operations in
its quest for a place in the public decision-making
process, the Hanafi operation was dissimilar from
most terrorist activity in its choice of targets.
Not only was the simultaneous seizure of three targets rare, perhaps only previously observed in the
September 1972 skyjacking by Palestinian terrorists
of three airplanes to Jordan's Dawson Field, but
the manner in which the targets were selected resembled a minor rather than a dominant theme of
terrorist activity. Only in a minority of cases do
terrorists select targets of specific symbolic value. Most target selections are highly indiscrimi
nate--a factor which tends to further intensify the
random aspect of terrorist violence.

The extent to which a target possesses symbolic
value is important to the leverage for negotiation.
Had the target selection been indiscriminate, there
perhaps would have been less room for negotiation.
The Hanafis struck out at symbols that not only
represented the perceived sources of inflicted
grievance, but that inherently incorporated a number of attitudinal projections. Some social sci-
entists call such symbols condensational symbols,
for their capacity to reduce to symbolic form a
number of attitudes and projected beliefs.[8] Attacking such a symbol provides a catharsis and in
some sense a political victory. The despised
source of grievance is publicly desecrated. The
desecration is transmitted by a far-reaching and
highly responsive media. There is no doubt that
these elements contributed to the Hanafis's perceptions that they had already won not just concessions from the larger socity but a symbolic
victory. If these motivations, and not vengeance,
were the real impetus behind the siege, then
Khaalis's lack of pursuit of the demand for authorities to hand over to him the five convicted Black
Muslims makes all the more sense. Those who sat at
the negotiation table quickly discerned, despite
the lack of a verbal or formal agreement, that
Khaalis had decided to capitulate. And why not?
The real purpose of the mission had apparently been
fulfilled. All that remained was the imminence of
death or capitulation. The thought of one's own
death grows tasteless when one has chewed on it for
thirty-eight hours.

THE VALUE OF NEGOTIATION

The importance of all of this is that it makes
a poignant statement, however indirect, about the
wisdom of our national government's public posture
of nonnegotiation. And I do not mean to suggest
that the conduct of negotiations in this case con-
tradicted that policy. For the conduct of negotiations was largely irrelevant to national policy,
as the major strategic and tactical decisions resided solely with the metropolitan police. They
had final decision-making and jurisdictional authority over the entire operation. The situation
does, however, demonstrate that negotiation in the
sense of bartering can lead to an appropriate solution that results in the freeing of hostages
without the authorities either outrageously compromising themselves or having set a series of
precedents that would make the next encounter more
likely or more difficult.

The value of negotiation becomes more evident
if we can assume that the rationale behind hostage
taking extends beyond the immediate calculation of
the likely capitulation of authorities to terrorist demands. If this is true--and the Hanafi situation as well as the tendency of terrorists to
seek publicity indicates that it is--then possessing or not possessing an avowedly firm policy on
negotiation may be largely irrelevant to whether
or how frequently a government is a target of
terrorist attack.

Terrorism is after all the political weapon
of the weak. A strongly armed, well-supported
group entertains not terrorism but guerrilla warfare or open conventional warfare as its means of
political conflict. (Terrorism when it does occur among relatively strong political groups is
an adjunct tactic rather than a strategy.) A weak
opponent does not have a reserve of people who can
be drawn upon for missions that continually end up
in destructive shoot-outs with authorities. This
factor is revealed in the terrorists' noticeable
penchant for what are called "soft" targets, and is
the justification the Israelis use for their tough
stand.

But there are yet other implications of dealing
with a weak opponent. A weak opponent is also an
opponent who needs a victory, even if it is only
face saving and symbolic. This means, as it did

in the Hanafi case, that there is much latitude for
governments to pursue in the context of the bargaining process.

This obviously is not an argument for a policy
of outright government capitulation, which unfortunately does occur in over 56 percent of the terrorist episodes. The West German government in
their dealings with the Baader-Meinhof gang eventually came to the conclusion that outright capitulation only stimulated further terrorist activity.
On 27 February 1975, during the West German elec-
tion campaign, the Baader-Meinhof gang kidnapped
Peter Lorenz, the mayoral candidate of the Christian Democratic Union. The West German government
capitulated to the terrorists demands, and five
terrorists were flown to Yemen in exchange for
Lorenz.

Apparently buoyed by this success, the terrorists struck the West German Embassy in Stockholm
on 24 April 1975, and seized eleven hostages and
demanded the release of twenty-six Baader-Meinhof
guerrillas and safe conduct out of the country for
them. This time the West German government supported by an aroused public sentiment refused to
capitulate. After twelve hours, the terrorists
set off a bomb in the embassy and tried to escape in
the confusion. One terrorist apparently committed
suicide, and the others were apprehended. One
hostage was killed, and several others and a dozen
Stockholm policemen were wounded.[9]

Even if the West German experience indicates
that outright capitulation encourages future attacks, there is no demonstration that a previously
announced position of intransigence, even when adhered to, is a deterrent. There are many observers who believe that it simply means that one side
is playing the game with all the cards sitting
faceup. The tragic deaths of U.S. diplomats George
Curtis Moore and Cleo A. Noel at Khartoum in March
of 1973 are taken as a case in point. There are a
number of State Department personnel who believe
that former President Richard Nixon's premature
announcement of the government's refusal to negotiate at the time that a "negotiator" was en route,
contributed to the terrorists' action.

The knowledge that the government will not negotiate for hostages has in addition led to a problem in morale among State Department personnel.
This factor is exacerbated by allegations that members of the department who have been hostages find
that they are viewed as pariahs because they are a

constant reminder of the potential vulnerability of everyone else. These appear to be subsidiary consequences of a policy whose primary utility and worth is undemonstrated. Under the best of policies such secondary consequences would warrant some reassessment of the primary value of the policy versus its negative consequences. In this case, the secondary consequences appear indicative of a price not worth paying.

Like the United States, Israel has maintained a consistently tough policy in dealing with terrorists. Its toughness may or may not have acted as a deterrent. As we noted earlier, Israeli officials claim that intelligence garnered from fedayeen terrorists indicates that the high risk to the terrorists growing out of Israel's policy is a deterrent to recruitment. Nonetheless, Israel remains a prime target of Arab terrorists despite its policy. Indeed, it would be naive to anticipate otherwise. The primary conflict of the terrorists is with Israel. Attacks against softer targets in the West, which for a long time were a major focus of terrorist activity, could be conceived as an alternate means to bring pressure on Israel. But it is only against Israel herself that the most symbolic and morale-enhancing victories are to be achieved. The necessity for such victories is well illustrated by the clamor and the accompanying embarrassment created by the spectacle of several fedayeen groups claiming credit for the same operation with the operation's accomplishments often being so modest as to require elaborate embellishments before being purveyed to the media.

As the Israeli experience indicates, the symbolic and media value of the target is of primary importance. If terrorism is theater, then terrorists want to perform where there are plenty of spectators in the galleries. Actions against the United States will receive major international media attention, and the United States is an embodiment of such an array of political symbolism that it can absorb the most distorted projections. The United States and her citizens stand as good primary targets. And this fate appears immutable to public pronouncements of policies that accept or reject the process of negotiation. We are such good targets that we are found as victims in over 50 percent of all terrorist episodes. And from 1968 to 1975 our government was the target of transnational terrorist demands as frequently as any other government on the globe, save Israel.

Although data indicating trends are terribly
sparse, from what cautious inferences are we able
to draw, the trend increasingly is for the American
government to become a target for terrorist demands.

All of this seems to say that the policy of
nonnegotiation has not achieved what it was designed to achieve. Of course, it may be argued in
some quarters that the situation could be worse.
Without the policy of nonnegotiation, we would have
incurred even more encounters with terrorists.
That is an interesting supposition, but one for
which unfortunately there is no evidence. The evidence we do have suggests that things are as bad
for our citizens and our government as for anyone
else.

Whether or not we are willing to negotiate, and
despite our stubborn inclination to publicize our
stance on such matters, it is clear that we are and
will continue to be a highly sought after target.
The policy has not created a deterrence, but it has
created some unanticipated effects.

The policy of nonnegotiation is a challenge to
the terrorists. A war of nerves is established between the nation-state and the terrorists. The
latter are inclined to escalate their tactical operations in order to find a point of vulnerability
where adherence to the policy will be broken. This
tends to mean taking "better" or more exotic hostages. This is generally a symbolic game where the
hostages are sought for their publicity value and
their symbolic testimony to the vulnerability of
the larger society. In such circumstances, there
is increased pressure on the government to negotiate.

The American policy was sharply challenged at
Khartoum with the taking of diplomats Moore and Noel
as hostages. A State Department "negotiator" was
dispatched. Whether or not the policy of nonnegotiation, reinforced by President Nixon's statement,
would have been adhered to is open to question. The
Tupamaro's seizure of the U.S. diplomat Claude Fly
in August, 1970, ostensibly did not result in negotiations. Fly's son, John, went so far as to ac-
cuse the Department of State of nearly getting his
father killed. Fly was released as an act of mercy
after he suffered a heart attack. The Tupamaros,
for their part, maintained that the Uruguayan government did enter into negotiations for Fly and an
Uruguayan national also being held hostage, despite
public disavowals by the government. If such nego-

tiations indeed did occur, it is doubtful that they
occurred without some consultation or orchestration
by the U.S. government.

When U.S. Ambassador Clinton Knox was seized in
Haiti in 1973, he was released the next day after
the Haitian government acting through French mediators paid $70,000 in ransom and gave twelve po-
litical prisoners safe conduct to Mexico. A demand
of $500,000 made on the U.S. government was turned
down. It was reported that the mediators themselves paid the ransom. The involvement of the
U.S. government was not made known, but it is highly doubtful that the U.S. government relinquished
complete control of the fate of our Foreign Service
personnel to another government.

These cases do illustrate that terrorists will
seize highly visible hostages in order to crack the
policy of nonnegotiation. As to the actual implementation of the policy, the sending of a "negotiator" to Khartoum,and the general disgust among
State Department people with Nixon's premature public announcement of nonnegotiation seems to indicate that the "negotiator" was being sent to do
more than appeal to humanitarian instincts. Moreover, all the above cases seem to indicate that it
is possible to negotiate, by using third parties
or by throwing the public responsibility on the
host government, and still maintain the fiction of
nonnegotiation.

NEGOTIATION AND POLITICAL CLIMATE

What a government does, of course, is contingent on what the political environment will accept.
The French government's tough stand against the
Croatian highjackers of a TWA domestic flight (September 1976) appeared to many Washington officials
involved in transnational terrorism to be indicative of the course of action that is possible when
there is no domestic constituency to which officials must respond. Had the Croatians actually
been armed, the precipitous French actions to shoot
out the plane's tires might have resulted in casualties. Despite a memorandum placed in the record praising the French for their cooperation, the
U.S. government was not consulted about the tactical steps the French were taking. While some officials have attributed this to technical problems
with radio communications, others have more than
hinted that the problems in communication had less

to do with technical difficulties than with
France's desire to implement a tough policy without
the intrusion of American concerns. The same tough
policy was not adhered to by the French in the Abou
Daoud affair. There France released and provided
safe conduct to the alleged architect of the 1972
Munich Olympics massacre of Israeli athletes. In
the latter instance, it was not pressure from the
domestic political constituency that resulted in a
softening of the handling of the terrorist, but
rather a response to the pressure of the Arab oil
producers and a desire to sell fighter planes to
Egypt.

The war of nerves between terrorists and governments is decisively played out against the
questions of political climate. What will the citizenry tolerate? As the targets are made more visible and possess greater symbolic value, the constituency will not be as likely to tolerate a hard
line. Even the Israelis found at Maalot (May 1974)
and later at Entebbe (July 1976) that there are
limits to what even a nation state under seige can
expect its citizens to accept.

At Maalot, the Israelis were confronted with
the prospect of refusing to negotiate at the cost
of the lives of children. Although accounts of
what actually took place at Maalot vary, one highly placed Israeli official who was there assured me
that the Israelis did enter into serious negotiations with the terrorists. The assault on the terrorists' position only took place after the terrorists refused to extend the deadline for negotiations. The negotiations were said to have been
complicated because of the involvement of third
parties requested as intermediaries by the terrorists, who were members of the Popular Democratic
Front for the Liberation of Palestine.

The Entebbe situation again presented the Israeli government with a situation where the citizenry raised opposition to the hard-line policy of
nonnegotiation. Indeed, it appears that the non-
military alternative was strongly considered until
the terrorists, in the course of negotiation, began to raise their demands. This is perceived by
negotiators as a sign that the other side cannot be
expected to live up to its end of the bargain.

The exotic target increasingly puts pressure on
a government to be more responsive to the citizenry.
Interestingly though, West Germany was able to move
to a tougher position in dealing with terrorists
after the kidnaping of Christian Democratic Union

mayoral candidate Peter Lorenz because that episode also moved public opinion in the direction of
a harder line. As the decision of whether or not
and how to negotiate is basically, if not ultimately, a political decision, it is also subject to
the forces in the political environment. It is
this situation that plays an important role in the
drama between terrorists and nation states, in the
former's selection of targets and the latter's selection of responses.

As political forces operate on the nation-state,
so too do they operate on the terrorists. The nation-state must maintain its relations with its
constituency, and the terrorists must maintain their
credibility. Negotiations consequently take place
not only in the context of the immediate environment but in anticipation of future environments.

At Khartoum, the Black September Organization
(BSO) still had on its mind the capitulation of its
members who had seized the Israeli Embassy in Bangkok in December of 1972. They had been persuaded
to leave Bangkok without their hostages and without their demands having been met. Indignant Thai
officials berated the terrorists for having precipitated an unseemly   event during a solemn national holiday, and caused the capitulation of the BSO
force. At Khartoum, there was concern for demonstrating that the BSO was still a force with which
to be reckoned, and that Bangkok had not established a precedent.

The impact of political considerations was also
revealed in the storm over the agreement reached
between District of Columbia Police Chief Maurice J.
Cullinane and the Hanafis. Cullinane in order to
obtain the release of the hostages worked out an
agreement whereby Khaalis and three of his followers
would be released on their own recognizance until a
grand jury indictment was produced. There were other stipulations in the conditions of release that
reduced Khaalis's freedom to virtual house arrest.
Cullinane drew fire from Senate Majority Leader
Robert Byrd (Democrat-West Virginia) and Senator
Lloyd Bensen (Democrat-Texas) as well as from local
Montgomery County, Maryland, Police Chief Robert J.
di Grazia. Di Grazia went so far as to argue that
hostage takers should be promised everything and
delivered nothing, as had been done in an earlier
episode that took place in Indianapolis.

Cullinane correctly noted that it was important
for the police to maintain their credibility. Indeed, it could be readily argued that much of what

goes on between hostage taker and negotiator in
any set of circumstances is ritualistic, and it is
important that both sides maintain their proper
roles in the course of the unfolding of the ritual.
In the next set of circumstances in which the District of Columbia police must enter into negotiations, the hostage takers will be assured that
agreements reached will be upheld, thus making the
ritual all the more viable.

NEGOTIATIONS AS RITUAL

     It is in the perception of the hostage scenario
as a ritual with subsidiary benefits to the hostage
takers resulting without complete capitulation by
authorities that the strategy of negotiation begins
to take on meaning and is comprehensible. To see
hostage taking as a plus-zero game where only the
authorities or the hostage takers can win is to reduce to a bloodbath a ritual that can otherwise
work out in exchanging face and political symbols
for human lives.
     To have said this, of course, is not to suggest
that all such encounters will end as well as the
encounter with the Hanafis. Certainly there are
situations, as Maalot and Entebbe appear to indicate, where the unfolding drama is less ritual than
double cross. In such situations, there can be no
substitute for the use of efficient and overwhelming force. Indeed, our domestic police have never
viewed hostage techniques, as refined and disciplined as they are, as a substitute for standard police methods, but rather as an extension of them.
Their success should at least give pause for some
reconsideration of the national government's policy
of previously espoused nonnegotiation. And the encounter with the Hanafis at least suggests that the
strategy and tactics used in dealing with criminal
hostage takers might not be altogether inapplicable
to situations in which the captors are ideologically motivated terrorists. After all, ideological rituals are still rituals.
     It is not so much that terrorists seize hos-
tages for the purposes of having only their primary demands fulfilled, for, in reality, these demands are often beyond what a sizable minority of
governments will concede. And those governments
that persist in not making concessions are no less
likely to be targets. Consequently, the terrorists
must have some other motivation. Indeed, if Dr.

David Hubbard[10] is correct in his assessment of the
terrorist as being unrealistic in his or her pursuit, and as not thinking beyond the point of bran-
dishing a weapon and unleashing the drama of the
moment, the likelihood of achieving the primary
demands is immaterial. What is important is the
process itself, the ritual, the assertion of self
by the individual terrorist or group. And in this
process it is secondary rather than primary considerations that are most important.

It is the fulfillment of parts of the ritual
that pave the way for the denouement of the scenario, the capitulation of the terrorist. And here
the concessions that are required can be trivial.
In fact, the concessions are vital for the terrorist to save face. Police officers in both America
and Great Britain agree that many concessions can
be granted that can make the terrorists feel successful without serving as a stimulus to further
acts of violence. It is such concessions that make
the drama worthwhile for the terrorists without im-
buing it with sufficient value or disgrace to warrant death.

The types of hostage situations that our federal government encounters overseas are not generally
barricade and hostage confrontations, although
Khartoum certainly was, and the future will undoubtedly hold similar encounters. The question
then follows as to whether or not the barricade
hostage situation has any lessons for the political
kidnapping. I believe it does.

Terrorist activities, after all, are the activities of those who have limited political resources. Consequently, there are a number of resource items that could easily be exchanged. As
Professor Singh has insightfully noted, one of the
primary functions of terrorist activity is simply
to put a grievance on the public agenda. This
means that acquiescence to simple demands for publicity might be sufficient to bring an encounter to
conclusion.

The resource needs of the terrorists would appear to suggest that there is a great deal of leverage for maneuvering in the course of the bargaining process. And the bargaining process itself
might very well be conceived as a ritual where the
terrorist group is making a presentation of self
in a quest for public and self-identity.

Some hitherto unrevealed aspects of the negotiations with the Hanafi leader Khaalis are illus-
trative of this presentation of self and the ritu-

alistic aspect of the negotiation process. The negotiations, it will be recalled, took place around
a folding table in the B'nai B'rith Building. When
Khaalis came down to negotiate he insisted that
District Police Chief Maurice J. Cullinane sit at
the head of the table. Khaalis addressed Cullinane
as general and had Cullinane address him with an
Arabic word meaning head of family. One of the
initial items discussed was the Hanafi demand for
the cessation of the movie Muhammad, Messenger of
God from the theater exhibition. Cullinane, following the generally desirable policy of being can-
did throughout the negotiations, informed Khaalis
that there was no way they could obtain anything
but temporary cooperations in having the movie
withdrawn from exhibition. Cullinane pointed out
that a temporary accomodation to the demand was at
best all that he could accomplish. Cullinane went
on to point out that the publicity from the seige
would more than stir a financial climate on which
the distributors would feel compelled to capital-
ize. Khaalis remarked that he understood this and
thanked Cullinane for what he had achieved and for
his candor. With that the negotiation concerning
the movie had ended.

The issue of the mass murderers that Khaalis
demanded presented to him for vengeance failed to
materialize in the end. One observer of this
scene wondered if it had ever been a real issue.

Preceding the discussion, there were other
aspects of the presentation of self and the creation of ritual that are so much a part of such
situations, for example, the manner in which
Khaalis determined how the two men would address
themselves and also the seating arrangement.
Khaalis requested that, in deference to the "general's" (Cullinane's) superior force, Cullinane
sit at the head of the table. Khaalis in the
course of making one of his demands then requested
a change of seating. That aspect in and of itself
was so symbolic that when the negotiations ended
without verbal conclusion, there was a sense among
the police and ambassadors that capitulation was
only a matter of time.

In any case study there is always the question
of representativeness. Is the incident truly representative of common aspects of negotiation episodes? Although the ritual and symbolic process
are to be observed in various aspects of terrorist-
hostage situations, a trained and experienced Israeli official asserts that the Hanafi episode has

little in common with a confrontation with an Arab
terrorist group. For such groups, he asserts, demands are demands and deadlines are deadlines.

Whether the differences are as striking as this
observer claims is questionable. Even among fedayeen operations there are few suicides, and even
among the few that exist there is always the question of whether explosives that blew a terrorist
apart were self-detonated, detonated by accident,
or in the course of the inevitable firefight with
Israeli troops. Further, there are few cases that
one can point to where the Israelis have really em-
barked on the ritual of negotiation. "Surrender or
die" is not just a tactic for the Israelis, it is
official policy. And Israelis perceive it as a
deterrent, especially to the recruitment of individuals for missions. This, of course, leaves us
with the empirical problem of an adequate test of
the symbolic ritual leading to denouement in cases
involving fedayeen.

Domestic police continually say that every case
is unique, and they wonder why the minuet leading
to denouement works so often. Yet one cannot help
but believe that human nature possesses enough
constancies so that fedayeen or hardened political
terrorists are not all that more willing to die
than are desperate felons or the Hanafis.[11] And
if terrorism is largely theater, entering into the
scenario might prove effective, irrespective of who
the actors are, although with greater or lesser
frequency. But one cannot help but feel that with
over four hundred negotiated episodes in New York
alone, without death, the ritualistic aspects of
hostage negotiation should not be easily discarded.

REFERENCES

1. Hannah Arendt, The Origins of Totalitarianism (New York: Meridian, 1962), especially, chaps.
11 and 12.
2. Kissinger's position as cited in Robert A.
Fearey, "International Terrorism," Department of
State Bulletin, 29 March 1976, p. 397.
3. From remarks made by Ambassador Heck to the
seminar on terrorism sponsored by the American Society for Industrial Security, Crystal City, Virginia, January 1977.
4. Fearey, p. 397.
5. Project ITERATE was designed and executed
by Edward Mickolus, Yale University. The author

wishes to acknowledge the assistance of Dr. Al-
fred Tuchfarber, Director of the Behavioral Sciences Laboratory (BSL), University of Cincinnati,
and Mr. Robert Oldendick of the BSL for providing
the data runs from project ITERATE. The ITERATE
data were provided through the offices of the
Inter-University Consortium for Political Research
(ICPR). Neither the BSL nor the ICPR bear any
responsibility for the use and interpretation of
the data. The author also wishes to gratefully
acknowledge the painstaking work of Edward Mickolus,
Yale University, who created project ITERATE.

6. Although it has heretofore not been made
public, the demand for the five Black Muslims was
not pursued with any consistency. This led to the
demand being interpreted by experienced negotiators
as not being serious. This perception of the demand indicates that the operation's success was
linked to symbolic rewards rather than to the
primary demands that were made.

7. From remarks by Professor Singh to the 1977
Annual Meeting of the International Studies Association, St. Louis.

8. For some standing examples of the use of
this concept see: Murray Edelman, Politics as Symbolic Action: Mass Arousal and Quiescence (Chicago:
Markham, 1971).

9. Major John D. Elliott, USA, "Action and
Reaction: West Germany and the Baader-Meinhof Guerrillas," Strategic Review 4, no. 1 (Winter 1976):
31-60. Major Elliot is considered to be one of the
most knowlegeable experts on the Baader-Meinhof organization.

10. "Interview with Dr. David Hubbard: The Terrorist Mind," Counterforce, April 1971, pp. 12-13.

11. On September 6, Superior Court Judge Nich-
olas Nunzio pronounced sentencing on the convicted
Hanafis. Khaalis was sentenced from 41 years to
123 years. The longest sentence was given to Abdul
Muzikir, who was responsible for the death of news-
man Maurice Williams. Muzikir was sentenced to 78
years to life. The shortest sentence was received
by Abdul Al Qawee, who held hostages at the com-
paratively placid Islamic Center. He was sentenced
to 24 years to life. Under the statutes of the
District of Columbia, the minimum sentence must be
served in full before release. Each defendant was
also sent to a separate federal prison in order
that no two would ever serve their terms together.

3
Hostage Negotiations and the Problem of Transference

INTRODUCTION

Frank Bolz is a garrulous jokester who embraces life with warmth, zest, and passion. He is, in his own inimitable way, a raconteur par excellence. He is a social being who thrives on the ambience of human interaction. Frank, a detective captain with the New York City Police Department, is its chief hostage negotiator. To date he has successfully negotiated, without loss of life, over several hundred hostage situations.

Many good experienced police in other cities will tell you in all candor and sincerity that the NYPD has gained a lot of mileage out of an especially talented individual. Frank, even with some discount for his tendency for modesty, will sincerely say otherwise. Talent is an undeniable and necessary ingredient in the repertoire of hostage negotiation resources. But beyond talent is a need for good procedures, training, and the ability to work in an environment where the political structure is supportive of the basic quest--success comes when everyone walks out alive.

Frank Bolz's role as comic and raconteur ends when he talks about hostage negotiation techniques. Frank is not simply a believer in hostage negotiation as policy; he is an active proselytizer. The record underscores his conviction. Wherever hostage negotiation techniques have replaced assault, the result is almost invariably the same--more people come out alive.

Before the initiation of hostage negotiation techniques, police relied on raw courage, stealth, and the assault. Many people died in those assaults. They still do. Recent figures released by the RAND Corporation[1] indicate that more hos-

tages die as a result of assaults than from direct
killing by terrorists. The assault does not appear to be a deterrent, despite its heavy cost in
life and limb. Countries in which the government
has refused to negotiate--Argentina, Colombia, Israel, Jordan, Turkey, and Uruguay--were nevertheless
targets of more hostage episodes.

Statistical evidence aside, the primary feeling
on the part of police negotiators is that assaults
are an absolute last resort. Assaults as a primary
strategy do not work; negotiations do.

As Lieutenant Richard Klapp, head hostage negotiation training officer for the San Francisco Police Department noted, "Negotiation is the most
compassionate, most humane and most professional
way to handle these things. We know that we have
saved lives and that is the way we know we have to
go."2

Men like Frank Bolz and Richard Klapp have set
a new image for the conduct of police work. Indeed, one of the most intriguing aspects of the
emphasis on negotiation is that it has redefined
the role and image within police departments of
good police work. This has meant a change in emphasis from physical tactics to psychological tactics. It has meant a redefinition, at least in
some quarters, of a good police officer. Negotiators emphasize such attributes as empathy, compassion, sensitivity, intelligence, and psychological insight as the skills of a good policeman.
They generally play down anything remotely indicative of the use of force. Negotiation replaces
physical prowess with intellectual skill and rep-
resents a set of values that--while not at variance
with all perceptions police maintain of their work--
is not universally adhered to in police circles.

The change in emphasis has also meant a greater
recognition of the reality of police work, empha-
sizing the kinds of skills police actually use
rather than some romantic image of the police. A
significant portion of day-to-day police work requires crisis intervention--breaking up a family
quarrel, keeping neighbors from fighting with each
other, or, as one Scotland Yard officer put it,
"Convincing people to do what is in their own best
interest" (said with a strong emphasis on convincing). Crisis intervention requires crisis negotiation, the skilled dialogue that substitutes in-
tellect and sensitivity for bravado. And just as
men reasoned logically long before Aristotle, police were engaged in crisis intervention and crisis

negotiation long before it was defined in such terms.

Despite the almost unparalleled success of hostage negotiation techniques, there is emerging in some public and even police headquarters a reaction against the policy of negotiation. Some of this grows out of a concern for the potential undermining of the strong, action-oriented image of police work. There is also concern that the rise in the number of hostage situations and the often spectacular drama in which they are enveloped is attributable to the contagion effect wrought by publicity and the reliance on negotiation instead of force.

In otherwise informed and sophisticated police and military circles, one hears bandied about, with hackneyed frequency, "If the Israelis can do it, why can't we?" This sentiment has taken on such proportions that I was recently asked by one metropolitan police department to assist them in informing the public as to the value and utility of negotiation. The sentiment for a policy based on containment and assault has recently found substanial support not only within the mass public that shares the perception that publicity and softness create hostage situations, but among rank and file police officers who perceive the assault is a deterrent and believe that current practices based on negotiation only play into the hands of terrorists and invite future episodes.

Such sentiments have no confirmation in fact. The impact of the press is debatable and is a subject that goes beyond the scope of this chapter. However, it might be worth noting that from 1973 to 1977, in virtually any week in any month, someplace in the world, someone was being taken hostage and it was being reported.[3] The so-called contagion effect is perhaps only a result of our sensitivity to the number of hostage situations given prominent play once a major episode makes the news. The argument that hostage episodes have increased over the past several years both in number and severity because of negotiations places the cart before the horse. It should be recalled that the tactic of negotiation came about after the rise in the number of hostage situations and the increase in their seriousness. The tactic of negotiation was developed in response to crisis and because the traditional mode of dealing with barricade and hostage situations resulted in casualties. Negotiations came about because police believed there had to be a better way.

HOW IT CAME ABOUT

On January 19, 1973, four formidably armed men entered John and Al's Sporting Goods Store in Brooklyn, New York. One man carried a sawed-off shotgun, the others handguns.

At 5:25 P.M., the police radio broadcasted a code 10-30 (robbery in progress) and thus began the chronicle of events that became known as the Williamsburg incident. It would last forty-seven hours and result in the death of one officer and injury to two others. Despite these unfortunate casualties, the Williamsburg incident began and ended as a model tactical operations that has been studied as an example worthy of emulation. It was meticulously planned, well executed, and illustrated the effectiveness of controlled fire power in the hands of a well-trained and disciplined tactical force.[4]

The quality of the operation was no accident. To a large extent, it was the result of work previously undertaken by a man whose role in the tactical scenario of hostage negotiations is little known, even in police circles. It was New York Police Department Chief Inspector Simon Eisdorfer who began promoting within the department the idea of an efficient tactical response to hostage situations. Eisdorfer's concern emanated from the tragic events of the 1972 Munich Olympiad, where an episode involving Palestinian terrorists who had seized Israeli athletes as hostages ended in the shocking death of all the athletes and several of the terrorists. Rightly or wrongly, it was the impression of many that the Munich police's tactical response was sorely inept,and that better training and contingency planning for such situations might have minimized the loss of life, if not prevented the tragedy entirely. As headquarters for the United Nations and as the seat of several consulates, New York appeared likely to be the scene of a terrorist incident.

Under Eisdorfer's stimulus, basic tactics were developed for using specially trained personnel to contain the scene and provide disciplined fire power. These tactics were later applied to the Williamsburg siege.

The Williamsburg incident, however, came on the heels of another dramatic hostage situation played

out in a Brooklyn bank and later captured for the
screen as Dog Day Afternoon. In response to the
succession of incidents, Police Commissioner Pat-
rick Murphy requested that a detailed policy and
methodology for dealing with hostage situations be
developed.

When the Williamsburg episode unfolded, Harvey
Schlossberg was a uniformed patrolman assigned to
a squad car. Patrolman Schlossberg, however, was
not a typical uniformed police officer. He held a
Ph.D. in clinical psychology, and when Commissioner
Murphy decided to develop a strategy for hostage
negotiations, Schlossberg's talents were recruited
to assist the process.

What Eisdorfer, in his role of commanding officer of the Special Operations Division, did for the
tactical procedures, Schlossberg would do for the
process of negotiation. By the time Schlossberg
finished developing, executing, and preaching his
plans for negotiation, officers in four hundred
American and Canadian police departments would go
about the procedures of hostage negotiation differ-
ently. The full impact of Schlossberg's work was
only beginning. Supported by grants from the Law
Enforcement Assistance Administration, law enforcement and military personnel from all over the free
world passed through the classrooms in the Emergency Services Unit Building in Brooklyn. Some of
Schlossberg's techniques found their way into the
policies and procedures of police in Great Britain,
the Netherlands, and West Germany. Even members of
the Israeli police passed through the school and
pondered whether the Israeli policy of nonnegotiation was indeed the only way to proceed.

The essence of Schlossberg's technique is to
establish communications and to keep communications
going for as long as it takes to get the subject to
surrender. In one incident in New York, it took
eleven days. Time is an expendable commodity--life
is not. There is much talk about throwing away the
clock, letting the dialogue progress, and directing
the captors into realizing that capitulation is
better than death. The underlying implication of
Schlossberg's technique is that time is generally
on the side of the authorities. (There has been,
recently, as a result of the experience of European
police and studies by psychologists of individuals
exposed to prolonged stress, some rethinking about
the impact of imminent confrontation with uncertainty and death on the mental health of the hostages. For this reason, among others, the Dutch

government decided to have its troops storm a train
and school where South Moluccans had held hostages
for almost three weeks in late May and early June
of 1977. This reassessment will be discussed be-
low.)

THE PROCESS OF TRANSFERENCE

The perception that time is on the side of the
authorities is based on the psychological concept
of transference, a mental process through which a
sense of closeness and attachment develops between
the hostage and his captor. As time wears on, both
captive and captor find themselves locked in a mutual fate. The captive feels powerless before the
captor, begins to identify with him, and perceives
that his hopes for survival reside with the captor.
The captor is seen as having the opportunity to
offer life to the captive--if only the authorities
will accede to the captor's demands. The fact that
the captive has been put by the captor in a situation where the captive's life has become a commodity of exchange is ignored. It is no longer the
captor, but the authorities who are perceived to be
at fault. The authorities are perceived to be
standing in the way of survival and holding out the
prospect of death.
The transference process is not necessarily
asymmetical. A similar bond can be created between
the hostage taker and the hostage. The impact of
sharing physical space under conditions of mutual
crisis and stress build intimacy and an emotional
bond that generally serves as a prophylaxis against
the hostage being killed. The strength of this
bond is said to increase with time. In fact, it is
commonly said among those experienced with hostage
negotiations that if a hostage is not killed during
the first fifteen minutes of an episode, the odds
are that he will not be killed.
There is yet another reason why time is perceived to be on the side of the authorities. As
the situation progresses and the prospect of imminent death continues, all but suicidally inclined
captors desire some way out of the situation.
Also, as time wears on, the police can rotate personnel. The hostage takers, unless well equipped,
trained, and in significant numbers, will find that
their capacity to act decisively and think clearly
will erode with time.

TRANSFERENCE AS A FUNCTION OF OTHER VARIABLES

The process of transference is not simply a function of time. It is also dependent on the nature of the interaction between hostage taker and hostage. All things being equal, the longer the period of time in which the interaction between hostage and captor take place, the greater the degree of transference. Time, however, is linked to the process of transference by the quality of the interaction. If the interaction is hostile, transference will generally not take place.

Interviews conducted by the Federal Bureau of Inverstigation with passengers on a Trans World Airlines flight skyjacked to Paris by Croatian separatists on September 10, 1976, illustrate the relationship between transference and the quality of interaction.[5]

One of the skyjackers, Marc Vlasic, was described as abusive, arrogant, and threatening. He had a penchant for fingering the phony dynamite brought on board in such a fashion as to add to the passengers' anxieties. Individuals who had substantial contact with Vlasic did not experience transference.

In direct contrast, the feelings of the passengers toward skyjacker Julie Busic, who was warm and outgoing while she played hostess to the passengers, were very positive. She was referred to by some of the passengers as "the perfect hostess."

Another one of the skyjackers, Petar Matvic, was also warm and positive in his reactions to the passengers who had contact with him.

Similar examples can be culled by contrasting the reaction of hostages in the first South Moluccan episode (December 2, 1975) in the Netherlands with the second (May/June 1977). In the first situation, there were several killings by the terrorists and at least one of the hostages was conspicuously abused. In the second episode, the hostages were relatively well treated until the assault by the troops when a terrorist deliberately killed one of the hostages. In the first South Moluccan episode, there were no reported incidents of transference. However, there were several in the second incident--a function of the difference in the quality of the interaction between captive and captor. Transference on the part of the hostages appears to be a selective process, contingent not

simply on the amount of time or the nature and degree of the crisis, but also (among other things)
on the quality of the interaction between captive
and captor. When the interaction is hostile and
negative, transference will probably not take
place. Moreover, when the interaction is not simply positive, but the captive actively seeks it
out, it appears that transference will be strong-
est.

Transference will generally not take place when
there are predetermined racial or ethnic hostilities between captive and captor. Israeli officials
inform me that there has not been one instance of
transference by an Israeli hostage toward an Arab
captor. Transference will also be precluded when
the hostage is capable of maintaining some intellectual distance, which enables the objective assessment of one's plight as having been wrought by
one's captors.

Richard Brockman, a twenty-nine-year-old psychiatric resident at New York's Columbia Presby-
terian Hospital,was abroad the ill-fated Trans
World Airlines Flight 355 when the Croatian terrorists seized it. In an article titled, "Notes While
Being Hijacked,"[6] he detailed his response to thirty terrifying hours on board the flight. At the
conclusion of the episode, the intercom blared and
Brockman recalled:

> "This is the captain speaking." His voice is
> clean, no cracks. "We have all been through
> an incredible experience. But it is over for
> us. No one is hurt. However, it is not over
> for our hijackers. Their ordeal is just be-
> ginning. They have a cause. They are brave
> committed people. Idealistic dedicated people.
> Like the people who helped to shape our coun-
> try. They are trying to do the same for
> theirs. I think we should all given them a
> hand."
> I look around me. The hijackers are
> smiling. The audience is applauding. It has
> come full turn. We arrive at the theater.
> Stop clapping, you fools. The cadence contin-
> ues. Tinker. Tailor. Actor. Fool. Let me
> out of here. Open the gate. Please let me
> out of here. No, the last curtain call.[7]

So, for Dr. Brockman, the episode came to an
end. And even in the surge of relief, he could not

develop the emotional affinity for his tormentors
that many of the other passengers did. To the end,
he was distant and objective, aware that his life
had been negotiated for some higher objective in
which he was only a participant as an accident of
circumstance.

Some additional items about transference also
emerged from the Croatian episode. In debriefing
passengers and crew, agents of the Federal Bureau
of Investigation noted that individuals who actively and consciously went out of their way to
interact with the terrorists were most likely to
experience transference. This is not to say that
transference was absent among other individuals,
but rather that it was most likely to take place
among those who sought it.

It appears from case by case observations that
a number of variables enter into determining
whether transference will take place: (1) the
length of time the hostage and captors are confined
(2) the quality of the interaction--Were the hostages well treated?; (3) the existence of predetermined racial or ethnic hostilities between hostage
and captor; (4) the predisposition on the part of
some hostages to seek out and relate to their captors.

The mechanism of transference that hostage negotiators like Frank Bolz and Richard Klapp rely
upon when the clock is thrown away is not always a
reciprocated relationship. Transference can and
often does take place on the part of the hostage
toward the captor without the sentiment being returned by the captor toward the hostage. In fact,
clever hostage takers have not been reluctant to
let the process of transference work to their own
advantage, nurturing transference among their captives while maintaining, behind outward signs of
friendship, a sense of deceitful manipulation of
the hostages. In the case of the first South Moluccan seizure of a Dutch train, one of the terrorists pointedly told the captives that he could
not kill any Dutch people because he was married to
a Dutch woman. This was not true.

One of the results of transference is that negotiators learn that they must be leery of trusting
hostages. Hostages can easily become unwitting ac-
complices of their captors, especially when transference takes place to the extent that the hostages
perceive police and not their captors as being the
primary obstacle to freedom.

Transference becomes an effective vehicle in

the process of negotiation when it is shared by
both hostage and captor. It is in those situations that throwing away the clock is effective.

THE STOCKHOLM SYNDROME

The process of transference was first noticed
as a result of a bank robbery in Stockholm. The
attempted robbery developed into a barricade and
hostage situation. During the course of the episode, a young woman hostage allegedly initiated
sexual relations with her captor. The motivation
was not response to fear or coercion, but an intimacy that developed as a result of sharing a common
fate in a situation of mutual crisis and the projected dependence of the woman captive on her captor. The relationship persisted after the bank
robber's incarceration.

FBI agents note that had observers been at-
tuned to the problem of transference earlier, the
syndrome would have been called Shade Gap syndrome
rather than Stockholm syndrome. Their reference is
to a kidnaping that took place in Shade Gap, Penn-
sylvania, in 1967. When law enforcement officials
came upon the kidnapper in a wooded area, he was
hurriedly walking to escape pursuit and encircle-
ment. A considerable distance behind him was the
kidnap victim, straining to keep up. The victim
had only to turn 180 degrees and walk off to freedom.

The most publicized episode of transference by
a hostage to her captors is that demonstrated by
newspaper heiress Patricia Hearst, who not only
took a lover from among her captors but also provided them with covering gunfire when they were
about to be seized for shoplifting. Patricia
Hearst's behavior was different only in degree from
what is commonly observed in hostages under long-
term stress. And if Patricia Hearst's responses
were more extreme, it is also true that the conditions of her captivity, both in terms of the severity of deprivation and duration, were also extreme.
These factors were probably exacerbated by her age
and lack of experience.

TRANSFERENCE AND HOSTAGE NEGOTIATION PERSPECTIVES

Time and intensity of the crisis can also function to promote transference between the hostage

negotiator and the hostage taker, which builds the
trust that eventually results in the hostage
taker's surrender. But even experienced negotiators succumb to the experience. One seasoned negotiator told me that in one situation he had developed such a close emotional relationship to the
captor that he found it difficult to testify a-
gainst him. The officer knew he had to do it and
he knew he would do it. However, before going into court he went to the subject and said, "_____,
you know I have to testify against you. I'm sorry
but it's my job." The subject responded by saying,
"Yes, I know. It's okay." The factors that enter
into the transference syndrome are also illustra-
tive of the dimensions that affect the likely outcome of hostage situations. These dimensions are:
(1) Who are the hostage takers and what are their
motives? (2) Who are the hostages? (3) What demands
are being made on whom?

WHO ARE THE HOSTAGE TAKERS?

    Although experienced police negotiators contin-
ually point out that each hostage episode is idiosyncratic, they are also quick to note that there
is a typology of hostage takers. Knowledge of the
type of hostage taker is important in determining
how the situation is to be handled. The most common type of hostage taker that the police encounter is the professional felon.
    The felon is basically uninterested in seizing
hostages. He usually takes hostages because his
escape route while committing a crime has been
blocked. The hostages appear initially to provide
an alternate means of escape. As time wears on,
they become a liability--the felon eventually comes
to grips with the reality of his situation. What
started out as armed robbery now has the potential
to become murder. Armed robbery is easier to face.
The felon only wants to be reassured that the massive phalanx of police that surrounds him will let
him capitulate without killing him. It is the task
of the negotiator to build the felon's trust to
where he will accept that reality. Felons are generally the easiest individuals to bring to capitulation. They are rational, did not initially seek
to take hostages, and want to spare themselves the
grief of a longer prison term for a more serious
offense.
    A more serious hostage taker is the psycho-

pathic individual who seeks to commit suicide but
is afraid. He embarks on a course of action that
he hopes will bring the police to the point of doing it for him. He is irrational and generally a
threat to the hostage and to himself. Often, in
this type of situation, negotiation may have to
yield to assault.

The political terrorist is generally viewed by
the police as the most threatening and dangerous
hostage taker. Police unfortunately assume that
political terrorists only embark on suicide missions. There is strong evidence to suggest that
this is not the case. Few terrorist missions are
suicidal. Most terrorist missions are against so-
called "soft" targets and embody fairly elaborate
escape plans. The threat of the political terrorist generally emanates less from his desire for
suicide than from his preparation, both mental and
physical, to take hostages and wait out the dialogue of negotiation. And, perhaps, the character-
istic that most distinguishes them from other hostage takers is the ability (somewhat reduced recently) of political terrorists to find some country willing to grant them sanctuary. This has been
a formidable weapon in the political terrorists'
arsenal.

In some intelligence circles, it is argued that
in part the more serious threat of the political
terrorist comes from the pressure of his colleagues
who, in his eyes, will not accept capitulation.
This conclusion must be approached with caution as
there have been sufficient instances of terrorist
capitulation to cast doubt upon this observation.
What is, however, more likely to happen is that as
the siege continues, dissension and conflict will
break out among the captors. Some members will
wish to continue the siege or even escalate the
violence, while others will seek a way out. Such
was the case in the Netherlands in late May of 1977
when a band of South Moluccan terrorists seized 170
hostages, including 105 children, in a train and
school.

The episode pitted noted Dutch psychiatrist and
negotiator Dick Mulder against twenty-four-year-old
Max Papilaya, the terrorist leader. After twenty
days, the Dutch government no longer found it could
go along with the policy of throwing away the clock
and resorted to an armed assault by specially
trained marines. The assault came about when, during the final forty-eight hours, the situation inside the train seemed to be falling apart. Papi-

laya's fellow terrorists were beginning to question
his authority. Papilaya showed signs of being willing to release the hostages while his comrades
were not. In the end, Mulder felt this internal
conflict would eventually obviate any chance for
successful negotiations.[8]

The possibility of internal dissension among
the terrorists cuts two ways. In the second Moluccan situation, the conflict led to the Dutch
government's use of force. In other situations,
the conflict has been adroitly exploited to lead
to capitulation. The fact that similar circumstances can lead to diametrically opposite results
illustrates how tenuous, fragile, and idiosyncratic
the process of negotiation can be.

One fundamental factor that is an important
determinant of the behavior of hostage takers is
that they have set out to purposely take hostages,
which indicates mental and physical preparation; in
addition, there was evidence in the course of the
second South Moluccan episode that the terrorists
now are assiduously studying the psychological procedures used by the police to negotiate for the
release of hostages. This is another important
factor that makes the terrorist hostage situation
difficult.

WHO ARE THE HOSTAGES?

Who the hostages are influences the terrorists'
actions against them The Hanafi Muslim (March 10,
1977; Washington, D.C.) episode illustrates this.
The Hanafis seized hostages at three locations: the
B'nai B'rith Building, the District of Columbia
Building, and the Islamic Center. At the B'nai
B'rith Building, some of the hostages were beaten
and tortured. At the district building, there was
similar physical abuse meted out and, there, in
addition, one man was killed and another was wounded. However, at the Islamic Center, where the hostages and hostage takers shared a religious bond,
the interaction bordered on being so cordial that
there was some initial concern as to whether any
useful court testimony would be obtained from these
hostages.[9] As is generally seen in the process of
transference, the quality of interaction between
hostage and hostage taker is the dominant factor in
building positive attachments. The nature of
interaction is determined by who the hostages are.
Thus, Israeli officials appear to be on rather firm

ground in their assertions that Israeli hostages
of Arab terrorists do not manifest signs of transference.

There is yet another aspect of the identity of
the hostages that will influence the final outcome.
It is widely believed that the more vulnerable or
the more prominent the hostage, the more likely a
government's response will be in favor of negotiation. Thus, even the Israelis are reported to
have negotiated in earnest for the children at
Maalot (May 15, 1974). The Israelis said they
could not conduct war over the heads of their children. Whatever a government does will largely be
influenced by what its populace will tolerate. A
nation is far and away more likely to tolerate nonnegotiation as policy when the lives being negotiated for are those of government officials than when
it is the lives of its children.

Beyond that, the taking of certain officials
who possess stature, visibility, and access to secret information will undoubtedly incur a response
from most governments indicating a willingness to
negotiate. Although former Secretary of State
Henry Kissinger (undoubtedly with great sincerity)
espoused a policy of nonnegotiation, few believe
that if he were taken hostage, the policy would be
adhered to.[10] Such factors, of course, mean that
the policy of nonnegotiation may ultimately be
little more than a stimulus for terrorists to seize
hostages for whom the government would be more
likely to negotiate--irrespective of espoused policy. The seizure of such hostages, however, is not
a guarantee that negotiations will take place.
There is the temptation on the part of any government, which can convince its citizenry of the wisdom of nonnegotiation, to avoid negotiation even in
highly visible instances where the character of the
hostages imposes an impetus for negotiation. For
in such circumstances, the inviolability of the
policy of nonnegotiation can be decisively demonstrated. Whether a government will, of course,
exercise or even confront such an option is another
matter entirely. There was strong opposition, in
some quarters of the populace, to Israel's stand of
nonnegotiation for the captives at Entebbe (July
1976) when that appeared to be the case.

WHAT ARE THE DEMANDS AND ON WHOM ARE THEY BEING
MADE?

It is my position that in those cases where the
primary demands can be deflected to the acceptance
of symbolic demands, as occurred in the Hanafi
Muslim episode, acquiescence of the terrorists to
symbolic victory is a possible way of achieving
denouement of the confrontation. There are, of
course, situations (the Baader-Meinhof operation
against the West German embassy in Stockholm in
April 1975 and the events at Maalot and Entebbe)
where it was extraordinarily difficult, if not impossible, to establish meaningful negotiations. In
Stockholm, the terrorists were unwilling to yield;
and at both Maalot and Entebbe, the terrorists
demonstrated bad faith by increasing their demands
once it was apparent that the Israelis were actually interested in negotiating. Between the extremes
of total capitulation, as the Black September Organization (BSO) demonstrated at Bangkok (December
1972) and the seemingly suicidal undertaking at the
West German embassy in Stockholm by Baader-Meinhof,
there may well be means for achieving accomodation,
without a government totally compromising itself
and appearing politically vulnerable and without
the terrorists completely losing face. The exposure of a government's vulnerability or the terrorists' loss of credibility can only lead to a hard-
ening of positions in the next encounter. The West
German government adopted a hard line in Stockholm
because of a previous total capitulation to Baader-
Meinhof when they kidnapped mayoral candidate Peter
Lorenz (February 1975), and the BSO adopted a hard
line at Khartoum after its prior capitulation in
Bangkok.[11]
In situations where the interaction between
terrorists and government is largely a means of the
terrorists' enactment of a ritual to gain access to
the public agenda, it is possible to obtain the
surrender of the terrorists without resorting to
force. The crucial factor is, perhaps, for such
rituals to become more institutionalized. Ritualistic violence, as practiced for many years by
Zengakuren (the Japanese leftist student group) and
the Japanese police, can sometimes take place within a strictly defined set of parameters. Zengakuren knew that they could not defeat the better
trained, disciplined, and equipped police.[12] The

police also knew that the task of subduing the students and engaging in combat, fought by both sides
with sticks and rocks, would be more or less formidable but would ultimately end in victory for the
police. The encounter was largely a ritual by
which the students made their demands known. The
police learned that the students could be beaten
but should not be beated so badly as to lose face
and consequently be forced to return once again to
the street in order to regain it.

Consequently, the type of demand made and the
context in which it occurs (that is, ritualistic
or nonritualistic) will provide or terminate opportunities for negotiation with the terrorists.

That, of course, is one perspective on the
subject. Israeli officials will strongly argue
that it is the wrong one. The political terrorists
they encounter appear to them to have little latitude to negotiate or compromise. Moreover, capitulation has consequences for them that are quite
different from those encountered by other types of
hostage takers. A political terrorist in Israel,
and many other countries as well, will end up in a
prison with other terrorists. If he is not put into prison and is sent home, he will invariably face
a court martial. As a result, there is a psychological frame of reference established that imposes
strong negative motivations to surrender. For
these reasons, the Israelis are adamant about their
general refusal to negotiate--a refusal that is
largely, although not wholly, immutable to considerations of who the terrorists and the hostages are
or what the demands are.

HOSTAGE COPING

The experience of being a hostage does not end
with the resolution of the situation. Many hostages relive the experience through daily psychological anxiety and sleepless nights. Studies are
currently underway both here and abroad to ascer-
tain how potential hostages might better cope with
the experience of being in captivity. Throwing a-
way the clock in negotiations may ultimately save
the most lives; but what will be the quality of the
life that is left? The longer the exposure to
stress, the greater the prospect of long-term psychological damage to the victims. It was, in
part, for this reason that after some twenty days
the Dutch government resorted to force to free

fifty-five hostages held by South Moluccan terrorists on a train in northern Holland. As Dr.
Dick Mulder, the government psychiatrist who negotiated with the terrorists was later to note, "How
long could they [the hostages] stand it without
longlasting physical and psychic problems?"[13] He
felt that after twenty days the situations had to
be resolved within the next week, in part, because
the stress was becoming unbearable for some of the
hostages.

Generally, the reaction of hostages to their
plight appears to be as varied as the personalities. Some hostages have long bouts of psychological stress afterward. If taken captive at work,
the work environment becomes so evocative for some
that they refuse to return to it. In one case in
New York, a woman even refused to pick up her pay
because it meant returning to where she worked and
had been taken hostage. One trained law enforcement officer who had been taken hostage in a cell
block described getting dressed in the morning to
go to work and being unable to go. Another officer
who had undergone the same experience in the cell
block claimed that after a full day's rest he went
back to work and suffered no adverse effects then
and has suffered none since. He further says that
he is slightly more cautious around the prisoners,
but fundamentally his behavior is the same. A woman who had been a hostage at Entebbe told me after
seven months she still awakens in the middle of the
night to the sound of the voice of the German woman
who had uniformly abused the hostages. Yet her
husband, who underwent the same experience of
captivity, claimed to have suffered no afteref-
fects. In Atlanta, Georgia, a bank holdup developed into a hostage situation and ended up with the
robber being shot in the presence of hostages. Yet
all the hostages returned to work.

The divergencies in response to the experience
of being a hostage appear to be indistinguishable
from the differences in responses to any form of
severe stress. It would appear that any study of
the responses of hostages to captivity would most
accurately be accomplished from the vantage point
of some baseline data. This would enable re-
searchers to assess the stress in the individual's
life prior to captivity.

Obtaining a suitable baseline may perhaps not
be as difficult as it appears. The number of hostage victims would appear to be extensive enough
so that a certain percentage would probably have

at some time prior to captivity undergone psychiatric examination. From the psychological records, baseline data would be established and responses to stress would than be assessed against such data. It would be very important to continue the observation of the hostage for several years to fully determine the impact of the experience and its lingering effects. It is conceivable, if the psychiatric experiences of concentration camp survivors is at all relevant, that the impact of captivity might not manifest itself for years. Etinger's[14] work on concentration camp survivors shows that some victims did not manifest responses associated with the experience until twenty years later.

There is some question as to whether it is useful to prepare hostages for captivity. Certainly, such a program would be of highly limited utility for the larger population, but could be of value to specific target populations such as high-ranking business executives, diplomatic personnel, and military officers stationed abroad.

If an individual is a potential hostage, there will generally be some indication of the increasing probability of the threat. Terrorists undertake detailed and extensive preparations prior to kidnaping prominent individuals. Such preparations provide signs of the terrorists' intentions (for example, surveillance or new and strange people suddenly showing up at or near the victim's home). From the vantage point of hindsight, many prominent hostages recalled incidents that upon reflection would have signaled them that they were being stalked as victims.

Prevention also requires changing routes to and from work and establishing patterns that make one a more difficult target. But even when that is all said and done, there is the likeihood that barring what some see as a suicidal "fire fight" with the terrorists, if one is willing to take the risks and invest the resources, virtually every potential victim can be confronted with the alternatives of acquiescing to captivity or choosing to be killed in an attempt at resistance. To some degree, then, captivity is virtually inescapable.

If this is a fair assumption, then for some people, preparing for captivity is as important as preparing to avoid being captured. This means that captives should realize what their own instinctive and natural reactions will be during captivity, what their captor will probably do to them, the re-

actions their captors expect, and what hostages
can do to counteract the psychological and phys-
cial pressure brought by their captors.

Terrorists use varying mechanisms to disorient
their captives. Generally, the captive will be
placed in an environment that precludes any sense
of time and space. This means that the individual
is not only cut off from contact with his loved
ones and the supportive elements of a familiar external world, but is also disoriented as to the
psychologically vital parameters of time and space.
This disorientation is aggravated by guards, who
may even torture the captive, and by isolation from
other prisoners.

If subjected to interrogation, the hostage is
also at a disadvantage. He will generally face a
skilled and experienced interrogator. Here the
process of transference can work decisively against
the hostage. Feeling totally dependent on the captor, the hostage's will might bend and yield completely. Again, we are reminded of the Patricia
Hearst episode. Her initial days of captivity exposed her to extreme sensory deprivation. She was
completely disoriented to the passage of time. Her
age and the ethically ambiguous circumstance of her
life in Berkeley's Telegraph district did not provide the strong set of ethics that makes one re-
sistant to manipulation by psychological transference.

As was observed in the case of American sol-
diers in the Korean war who were subjected to psychological manipulation by the Chinese communists,
individuals with strong belief systems were highly
resilient to brainwashing techniques. In contrast,
those whose beliefs were open and flexible were far
and away more likely to submit to indoctrination.[15]
In two well-known hostage incidents, involving the
capture, by Uruguayan Tupamaros, of Dr. Claude Fly,
an American agronomist, and British Ambassador
Geoffrey Jackson, the individuals not only resisted
psychological manipulation but were of such firm
character that they began exercising a strong influence over the guards. The terrorists found it
necessary to remove some of the guards who had
fallen under the prisoners' influence. For, as
Dutch psychiatrist Dick Mulder has noted, some of
the toughness and anger of terrorists in the initial moments of a takeover are an attempt to deal
not only with their fear, but also with their guilt
at having seized innocents.[16] Both Fly and Jackson
worked at breaking down the hostility that their

guards held towards them.[17]

Both Fly and Jackson were men of strong religious conviction (Fly even wrote a book on Christian ethics during his captivity). Both men had strong family ties, had achieved a degree of personal success in their professional lives, and understood how their captors were attempting to manipulate them.

One of the greatest difficulties with any alien situation is the inability to find the psychological anchors that we all require in order to deal with life. Uncertainty, as a number of students of man and his interaction with his environment have observed, is a most difficult and anxiety ridden circumstance. The degree of anxiety produced in such situations is said to be so great that even situations that produce clearcut negative expectations are perceived as being easier to manage.[18] The benefit derived from preparing for captivity is to no small degree found in the reduction of uncertainty. The captive can anticipate and understand what his captors are doing and what is likely to follow. To the extent that this is possible and that the process is reinforced by the hostage having made accurate predictions, the level of uncertainty, disorientation, and anxiety is sharply reduced.

It is also important for the individual to make some mental link to the outside world. Sir Geoffrey instructed his wife to return to England in the event of his captivity and to paint the interior of the house. She was further instructed as to the sequence in which the rooms were to be painted. This provided him with a picture of what she was doing on each day of his captivity, and it provided him with a link to her. It is also important that a captive engage in physical and mental exercises. This contributes to maintenance of mental and physical health during confinement. Sir Geoffrey wrote children's stories and followed the Canadian Air Force Exercise Program. Although his captors took his writing materials away, Sir Geoffrey persisted by writing in his head and published his work shortly after his release. Dr. Fly wrote a book on Christian ethics while in captivity. His own conduct during his ordeal was so in accord with the principles he espoused that even the terrorists referred to him as a saint.

The Tupamaros released both men, Fly because of his ill health and Jackson following a triumphal jail break by 106 political prisoners. The

latter episode served as a major propaganda victory
for the Tupamaros.

As in most such cases, the captives were pawns,
used for propaganda and to wrest concessions from
the government. Most terrorists do not desire to
kill preselected prominent hostages, unless the
hostages were specifically seized as targets for
assassination. (The seizure and subsequent assassination of the American policeman Dan Mitrione
who was assigned as a consultant to the Uruguayan
police is a case in point). It appears that there
is a reasonably good chance that a hostage will be
released even if the demands are not acceded to;
however, there is some controversy over this point.
The Tupamaros claim that the Uruguayan government
had, in fact, entered into negotiations for the release of Fly. Whether anything came of these alleged negotiations was not revealed. Observers
generally argue that it is reasonable to assume
that if a specifically selected individual is seized as a political hostage and not executed shortly
thereafter, then he most likely will not be executed. When execution is decidedly going to be
carried out, it is usually done swiftly and publicly without negotiation being entertained. After
all, the execution of a publicly visible individual
renders a different type of political statement
than the seizing of a hostage for the purpose of
gaining concessions from a government.

HOSTAGE COPING: THE MASS PUBLIC

It may be useful for individuals who are especially vulnerable to becoming hostages to prepare
themselves for being taken captive and for facing
treatment by captors. Such preparations, as pro-
cedural mechanisms, are peripheral to the interests
of the mass public. But the public is involved in
any politically salient hostage situation. Targets
are selected because they can be used to threaten
public authority and public safety. Terrorism by
definition is an act that seeks to influence a
population significantly larger than the immediate
target. Thus, the quality of the public's understanding and its response to terrorism of all va-
rieties is highly significant. Ultimately, it is
public opinion in a democracy that will help shape
the political environment within which government
officials must act.

As Dr. Frank Ochberg has noted:

A public which overreacts in outrage against
the victim's helplessness may precipitate
harsh, simplistic counter terrorist measures.
A public which joins the victim in identify-
ing with the terrorist-aggressor may under-
mine the morale and confidence of the police.
A public perplexed and alienated by the entire process may interfere with the bond of
trust between government and governed which
is necessary for the survival of democratic
institutions. But, on the other hand, a
public that is reasonably well aware of the
repertoire of human responses which are effectively used by men and women under stress-
even under the stress of terrorist threat and
captivity -- such a public will be able to
participate in rational decision making a-
bout national policy on terrorism.[19]

Dr. Ochberg's point is well taken. Too often
the public implications of the terrorist act are
ignored. Worse, yet, the terrorist's victim is
generally a substitute for the state, but few nations assume any responsibility for their citizens
who become the unwitting victims of terrorism. The
effects of the experience of being victimized by
terrorists extend beyond the mere time in captivity. Psychological problems tend to persist,but our
society generally does not wish to assume responsibility for them. In addition, it is alleged that
there is a lack of concern by some governments for
employees who have been taken hostage because of
their role as representatives of government. U.S.
Department of State employees who have been taken
hostage allege that there is a bureaucratic in-
sensitivty to their plight. They have become pa-
iahs because their very presence is a reminder to
others of everyone's vulnerability to terrorism.
These same individuals further add that their
careers have, as a result of their ill fate, reached a trajectory, and there is no promise of ad-
vancement. These allegations, if true, coupled
with the formal policy of nonnegotiation, are said
to have an adverse influence on morale in the U.S.
Department of State.
The fact, however, that such issues have come
to the public's attention indicates at least a
concern about the policy and initiative toward
change. Certainly, developing tolerance in the
mass public for the plight of victims is not likely
when a governmental agency whose employees are the

target of terrorist activities is not responsive
to the ensuing difficulties of its own employees.
     The government may not have such control over
the image of terrorism conveyed by the popular
media. After all, terrorism is news and the media
is there to convey the news generally in a form
that sells copy. However, the government can make
the public aware of the difficulties and problems
faced in hostage situations. In this way, the public, while not exposed to the same information with
which potential targets are provided, will have
access to sufficiently high quality information
that discussion can take place in an informed manner, leading to the type of environment that as-
sists in maintaining intelligent and objective responses to a problem too easily caught up with e-
motional fervor. Such discussion, hopefully, will
lead to a less vindictive response toward hostages
who are compromised by the process of transference
and to the establishment of public attitudes that
will recognize that extinguishing liberty in the
rush to combat terrorism only accomplishes for the
terrorists what they are unable to accomplish for
themselves.

REFERENCES

     1. Brian Jenkins, Janera Johnson, and David
Ronfeldt, "Numbered Lives: Some Statistical Ob-
servations from Seventy-seven International Hostage
Episodes" (Santa Monica: The RAND Corporation, July
1977).
     2. From a personal interview with Lieutenant
Richard Klapp, January 28, 1977. See also Ralph
Craib, "Crisis Negotiators in Hostage Cases," The
San Francisco Chronicle, January 29, 1977, p. 2
     3. M. Jane Stewart, "Hostage Episodes, 1973-
1977: A Chronology" (unpublished).
     4. The depiction of the Williamsburg incident
is from personal interviews. See also John A.
Culley,"Defusing Human Bombs--Hostage Negotiations,"
FBI Law Enforcement Bulletin, December 1974 and
Donald F. Cawley, "Anatomy of a Siege," The Police
Chief, January 1974.
     5. I am indebted to Special Agents Conrad
Hassel and Thomas Strentz of the FBI Academy for
their insights on the process of transference.
     6. Richard Brockman, "Notes While Being Hi-
jacked," The Atlantic, December 1976, pp. 68-75.

60

7. Ibid., p. 75.

8. "Psyching Out Terrorists," Medical World News, June 27, 1977.

9. The Hanafi episode is described by Abraham H. Miller, "Negotiating for Hostages: Implications from the Police Experience," (paper presented to the International Studies Association, March 1977).

10. Kissinger's position as cited by Robert A. Fearey "International Terrorism," Department of State Bulletin, March 29, 1976, p. 397.

11. On March 2, 1973, three diplomats--two Americans and one Belgian--were murdered in the Saudi embassy in Khartoum by agents of Black September after an official announcement,by President Richard Nixon,of the U.S. Government's refusal to negotiate. The announcement came while a U.S. Department of State negotiator was enroute. Many observers have concluded that the action taken by Black September was to demonstrate that their capitulation in Bangkok was not typical of their pattern of operations.

12. Michiya Shimbori, "The Sociology of a Student Movement-A Japanese Case Study," Daedalus, Winter 1968.

13. "Psyching Out Terrorists," p. 17.

14. Leo Etinger remarks to the Fourth International Seminar on Terrorism, sponsored by the Centr International de Criminologie Comparee, Evian, France, June 1977.

15. E.H. Schein, Winifred F. Hill, H.L. Williams, and A. Lubin, "Distinguishing Characteristics of Collaborators and Resisters among American Prisoners of War," The Journal of Abnormal Social Psychology, 1957, vol. 55, pp. 197-201.

16. "Psyching Out Terrorists."

17. U.S Congress, Senate, Committee on the Judiciary, Hearings on Terrorist Activity, Hostage Defense Measures, 94th Cong., 1st sess., July 25, 1975.

18. In this regard, see Ivo K. Feierabend, et al., "Social Change and Political Violence: Cross-National Patterns," in The History of Violence in America, Hugh Davis Graham and Ted Robert Gurr, eds. (New York: Bantam Books, 1970); and Abraham H. Miller et al., "The J-Curve Theory and the Black Urban Riots," The American Political Science Review, vol. 71, no. 3 (September 1977), pp. 964-982.

19. Frank Ochberg (remarks to the Fourth International Seminar on Terrorism, sponsored by the Centre International de Criminolgie Comparee, Evian, France, June 1977).

4
SWAT (Special Weapons and Tactics):
The Tactical Link
in Hostage Negotiations

INTRODUCTION

When a situation calls for extraordinary weapons and tactical support that cannot be provided by the regular police patrol, a specially trained and equipped unit is called to the scene. Such units are called "barricade squads," "emergency service units," "advance teams," and so forth. The most common name is "SWAT" (Special Weapons and Tactics) teams. Owing to a conscious attempt on the part of some police departments to downplay anything that resembles a military operation and owing to a strong desire to avoid being linked to the dramatizations of police work portrayed in the television program "SWAT," this name has been formally eschewed in a number of departments. It has been replaced with what are considered to be more publically palatable euphemisms. Yet, the notion of a special weapons team clings, and even where a euphemism has been substituted, officers talk about the special weapons unit. For this reason, I have referred to such units as special weapons or SWAT units, even though in any particular case, a department may have gone to great lengths to call the units by another name.

What follows is a discussion of some of the more prominent of these units and how they operate, the kind of tactical support they provide in hostage situations, and some of the issues that surround their operations. These observations are based on in-depth interviews with team leaders and members, close observation of a team in action, public reports in terms of film and media, and internal police reporting of specific incidents.

For several reasons, I avoided a city-by-city comparison of procedures. Most procedures are

sufficiently similar so that distinctions are often
of little practical significance. Moreover, I felt
that such comparisons have the appearance of being
invidious. Instead, I sought to highlight a procedure that appears to exemplify a given concept or
tactic.

Some readers will be disappointed, inasmuch as
incidents--even those described by the press--are
alluded to without specifics. This was necessary
to preserve the anonymity of respondents and because what happened is far and away more significant
than where it happened and under whose authority.
Disclosure of the latter information of necessity
results in defensiveness and little learning. Police departments are always vulnerable to political
intrusion. Police journals have a deliberate penchant for describing and analyzing good operations--
such are the dictates of politics. Bad operations,
however, also have a contribution to learning that
is worthy of study and reflection. This can only
occur when the parties involved are spared the need
to be defensive. Consequently, even some operations that received formidable publicity are ana-
lyzed without reference to time and place.

THE PHILOSOPHY OF SWAT

"What we do is take a man who is oriented to
act on his own and bring him into a situation
where he acts in a team. He is trained not to be
impulsive, but rather to act only when he is told."
In that statement, a highly placed Washington, D.C.,
police official described the essential philosophy
behind the special weapons and tactical units police have developed to deal with hostage and barricade situations.

If there is one common attribute in the personalities of the men and women who join the police,
it is that they are action oriented. To be out
there in the street where the action is taking place
is the guts of police work. This is a commonly and
repeatedly cited comment that came across in my
interviews with police in various ranks and in various cities. What the special weapons units have
done is to harness that individual ethic and bring
it into an organized, effective, and well-disci-
plined team effort.

The single most important aspect of a special
weapons team is discipline. This is inculcated
through intensive training and buttressed by highly

selective recruitment. It is further reinforced
by a large number of officers on a team and a high
ratio of supervisors to team members. In New York,
the ratio of supervisors to personnel runs one to
four--sometimes, even one to three. As one New York
police official put it, "We impose a lot of supervisors because we are dealing with a lot of firepower and that firepower is useless, even detri-
mental, unless it can be controlled."

The concept of discipline and controlled firepower is so basic to the special weapons operation
that there has been a general disdain on the part
of all the special weapons personnel I have interviewed toward the TV program "SWAT." The program,
which is set in Los Angeles, is a fictional depiction of the operations of the Los Angeles Police
Department special weapons unit. Unfortunately, a
segment of the audience was unable to distinguish
between reality and fiction. In the minds of some
of the audience, the TV "SWAT" program was insepa-
rable from the operations of the Los Angeles Police
Department. The Los Angeles Police Department received hundreds of letters asking for autographs
from the various fictional characters in the show.
To a large extent, the portrayal created an erroneous and improper conception of the nature and
function of special operations units. As one
officer in the Washington, D.C., police department
noted, "We don't jump out of trucks and start killing people. There are more rounds fired on TV in
five minutes than we fire in years."

Beyond the depiction of the special weapons
unit as jumping out of trucks and killing people,
many police objected to the portrayal of the unit
as sitting around waiting for the next dramatic
hostage or barricade situation to unfold. In real
life, such units are assigned to anything from
routine police work to special duties. The assignments vary with the needs of the local department.
In the larger metropolitan areas, such units are
drawn from members assigned to special operations
work, such as the Emergency Services Unit of the New
York Police Department, which does everything from
rescue work to extrication of corpses.

The most dramatic contrast to the media and
popular version of "SWAT" is the definition the
police use of a successful operation. This is one
in which the problem is brought to an end without
casualties or loss of life--and that means the lives
of the perpetrators, as well as those of the victims. Interestingly, this definition of success is

widely adhered to by the police. One of the strong-
est resentments articulated by members of the Los
Angeles Police Department SWAT team was against the
cliche bandied about in police circles that if a
person takes hostages in New York City, the police
will talk the person to death, while in Los Angeles,
the police will shoot the person to death. This
erroneous and negative image of the Los Angeles
Police Department operation is unfortunately so
widespread that it is even held by members of other
California police departments.

In point of fact, the current Los Angeles Police
Department hostage negotiation operation is only
different from that used by the New York Police Department inasmuch as some negotiators are directly
assigned to SWAT and are not part of a separate
unit. The advantages and disadvantages of this procedure are a subject of debate in police circles.
The New York position is that the negotiator must
be as "neutral" as possible. This is reflected in
the decision of New York Police Department Chief
Negotiator Frank Bolz to conduct negotiations in
civilian clothes. This is also the position of
Lieutenant Richard Klapp, head negotiator for the
San Francisco Police Department.

HOSTAGE NEGOTIATORS AS SWAT MEMBERS

From the perspective of neutrality, negotiators
as part of the SWAT operation are seen as being in
role conflict. After all, negotiators maintain,
while the basic definition of success is the same
for both special weapons teams and negotiators in
hostage situations, one cannot escape the fact that
the special weapons units are primarily action oriented. Their training is geared toward the controlled use of tactical and strategic firepower,
where objectively success means that no shots are
fired or shooting only takes place under specific
conditions. Despite objective definitions of success, subjectively, many negotiators argue that
there is a strong desire on the part of every person to fulfill the mission for which he or she is
trained--like the Israeli pilots who flew the
Entebbe mission. When they were asked how they felt
about being given the green light, they responded
by noting that they had trained so long and so hard
for such a mission that there was a great excitement in having the opportunity to execute it. Negotiators further maintain that in contrast to SWAT,

the objective and subjective fulfillment of their
mission resides in the same result--talking the perpetrator into surrendering.

The SWAT personnel, however, propose that such
distinctions between subjective and objective fulfillment of one's role may be more true in theory
than reality. After all, they propose, even the
New York Police Department negotiating team maintains its strong skills in marksmanship should a hot
pursuit situation arise out of a hostage situation.
Moreover, while SWAT teams are action oriented, a
good SWAT team is robotlike in its response to discipline and to its commitment that a successful operation is one in which a resolution is brought a-
bout without casualties or injuries to any of the
participants--including the perpetrator.

It is further argued that having negotiators as
part of the team is perhaps a response to the reality of police work--inasmuch as there are a large
number of negotiations that are quickly brought to
a conclusion by police arriving on the scene. These
situations, being more common and less dramatic, do
not make the headlines but constitute the bulk of
police negotiations. Denver police inform me that
their situations seldom last long enough for the
negotiators to get to the scene--de facto, the negotiations are done by the SWAT team. Similar observations were also communicated to me by members of
Scotland Yard, who noted that most negotiations are
undramatic, of short duration, and accomplished by
the beat patrolman. These observations lead one to
conclude that the motif of crisis intervention is
such a large component of police work that hostage
negotiation training might be made more generally
available, but this does not answer the question of
how the more dramatic and long-term negotiations
should be handled. Should negotiators called upon
to perform in such situations be tactically part of
a special weapons team, or should they be a separate unit?

Scotland Yard, in part, justifies their decision to use separate personnel on tactical grounds.
Their weapons people are drawn from the weapons
specialists at the Yard's academy. They work and
train as a unit. Negotiators are generally drawn
from the antiterrorism squad. They, in turn, will
be more knowledgeable about the personalities and
operations of the people likely to precipitate
serious hostage situations. There appears to ac-
crue here a natural division of labor based on
training and work experience. Moreover, since none

of the negotiators are armed and since all the
negotiators are in civilian clothes, this means that
any civilian in the controlled inner perimeter who
is in fact armed is a perpetrator.

IMPLICATIONS OF THE DIVISION OF LABOR

Irrespective of the decision as to whether or not
a fairly strict division of labor is created between special weapons personnel and hostage negotiators, one pattern that clearly emerged in some
police departments that had separated negotiators
from the weapons personnel was a lack of sufficient
contact between the units to provide the best possible understanding of each other's roles. In one
department, the negotiating unit perceived that the
special weapons people had created what might have
developed into a crisis in one hostage situation by
placing personnel on a rooftop which the negotiators
had ordered cleared as part of the exchange with
the perpetrators. In my interviews with the negotiators, this incident was discussed with strong
concern and alluded to as confirmation of the un-
professional mentality of some of the special weapons people. Actually, the incident was precipitated by two regular policemen, who on their own
initiative had sought to establish a tactical ad-
vantage--and almost destroyed the credibility of
the negotiators in the process. Since there is
some mutual distrust between the negotiators and the
SWAT unit--as there invariably will be in all separate units in any organization--the erroneous perceptions have not been resolved. One means of
attacking this problem is to have elements of both
units together during debriefings. This unfortunately is not always done.

In any situation where there is a creation of
special units with complementary assignments, there
is bound to be friction. Noteworthy throughout the
interviews with some departments with separate
hostage-negotiating and SWAT operations was the
lack of knowledge the members of each unit tended
to demonstrate concerning the training and operations of the other unit. Basic information on the
recruitment and training of the other unit was
sometimes absent. Negotiators seemed to be un-
informed about the internal operations of the special weapons personnel and vice versa. This a-
gain appeared to be a problem that could be readily
alleviated by better communication and joint de-

briefings.

OTHER CONFLICTS AND MEANS TO AVOID THEM

The basic organizational conflict emanating from the creation of SWAT units is the internal rivalries and jealousies that any elite unit generates. Although these conflicts are inevitable, there are mechanisms that have been adopted which ease the severity of conflict. New York, Los Angeles, and San Francisco, for example, have refrained from providing special weapons personnel with extra pay. New York has also removed the special weapons personnel from making any arrests. As one New York police official put it: "If we make some arrests and not others, they will say we only take the good ones. If the responding officers know we make 'collars' they will be less likely to call us when we are needed. We avoid the problems by not making any arrests. We turn the perpetrators over to the responding officers. It is their 'collar'-- all the time."

In San Francisco, where the SWAT unit does make arrests, the underlying philosophy is still the same-that arrests will be made whenever the team responds and is in a position to make the arrest. There is to be no selectivity in determining which arrests will be made by the team and which will be made by responding officers. It is a question of who is in a position to do it. As a San Francisco Police Department special weapons officer put it: "We respond to anything we can, and we take all the arrests. That way, it cannot be said that we just take the good ones. This stops the animosities." Members of the San Francisco team further point out that they share the publicity with other units. This factor, and the absence of extra pay, they claim, are formidable aspects in restraining hostilities and jealousies between the rest of the force and an elite unit.

Resentments, however, are inevitable. Even without extra pay or arrests, SWAT is an elite unit, with more individuals wanting to join than there is space available. In Denver, for example, which has a total police force of 1,200 men and a SWAT team of 25 men, there are currently 200 applicants waiting for a position on the SWAT unit. Although Denver does provide extra pay to its team members, a similar demand for a position with SWAT can be found in any major police department.

RECRUITMENT AND TRAINING

Getting on the team anywhere is not easy. In
Denver, there is a five-year minimum experience
qualification, a physical requirement, and a demand
for reliability and strict submission to discipline.
After making the Denver team, an individual must
be prepared for a strenuous morning of running, cal-
isthenics, and physical conditioning. In addition,
there is one full training day per month. This
can include anything from practice assaults to gas
drills. While experience, reliability, and submission to discipline are the primary ingredients in
all special weapons teams, the emphasis on physical
conditioning varies greatly. In some departments,
there is no special physical conditioning requirement, while in others, such as in Chicago, there
is a special emphasis on maintaining the special
weapons personnel in a state of excellent physical
readiness.

The Chicago program is largely the result of the
direction of Commander Walter Valee. Under the
tutelage of the Chicago Bears' athletic trainer,
Commander Valee's special weapons teams are trained in aerobics and isotonics three days per week.
The men who apply for the special weapons teams
are generally found to be athletic and in good
physical condition. Yet, there is usually a division of activity between the men. Some are found
to be involved in isotonic-type exercise, while
others are involved in aerobics. What the Chicago
program does is to cross-train the men so that all
are equally proficient in isotonics or aerobics.
The program is highly demanding, and the men are
tested every six weeks.

The function of the program is not simply to
put the men in a state of physical readiness, which
is vital to the demands of their occupation, but to
develop the men's cardiovascular system to the point
where the heart beat is lower under stress. The
men are run and made to shoot after coming to a
halt--with pulse rate increased. This firing under
stress simulates real life conditions, and the
athletic programs make the men more tolerant of the
physical and emotional stress they are likely to
encounter in real life situations.

The Chicago program, like many of the others,
is supplemented with such training as night assaults, shooting and assaults under different

weather conditions, and "hostage" shooting. Hostage shooting is accomplished against a double silhouette where one silhouette is imposed over another. Marksmen must qualify by being able to hit only the second (nonhostage) silhouette.

In San Francisco, specialized training sessions are generally undertaken by teams at least once a month. These often are done in competition with neighboring departments and under the supervision of the FBI. Praise for the FBI in taking an active role in such training was very strong. Members of the special weapons teams saw the FBI as playing a vital role in providing new training techniques and also in making possible joint operations, since the team trained with the FBI and relied on similar tactics.

SWAT TRAINING AND ITS IMPLICATIONS FOR NEGOTIATION PROCEDURES

One of the problems that appears to ensue from having an excellent special weapons operation where negotiators are part of the team and under its direct tactical control is that the training emphasis appears to be primarily on the weapons component of the team mission. In contrast, when one interviews a separate negotiating unit, one hears a great deal about the process and techniques of negotiating. There is even a concern for academic learning in psychology and behavioral sciences and how work in these disciplines might better assist the negotiators in their handling of subjects. Moreover, while SWAT teams spend training time on assaults and physical conditioning, negotiating units spend time simulating hostage situations, studying tapes from previous operations, and attending seminars that contribute to the enhancement of their negotiating skills. Since the hallmark of virtually every special operations team is that every man qualify for every position--except in some cases that of marksman--this puts a double load on the hostage negotiators assigned to SWAT. They must maintain their special weapons skills and still maintain their negotiation skills. It is obvious that the demands to maintain both functions in top condition are too great for any single individual. Moreover, if an individual is a negotiator and also a member of a special weapons team, the primary ethos to be found among his peers and co-workers will be one that places an emphasis on the profi-

ciency of the action-oriented activities of the
team. Consequently, the maintenance and updating
of negotiating skills will of circumstance, and
perhaps necessity, take a secondary place to the
demands for maintenance of skills more directly
related to the operations of the special weapons
units.

There is another aspect of the special weapons
operation that appears to reinforce the deemphasis
on negotiation. At the bottom line, when all is
said and done, even many experienced and sophisticated police negotiators believe that for the
overwhelming majority of their experiences that
involve interrupted felonies where hostages are
seized as an afterthought, the primary role of the
negotiator is invariably and eventually to convince
the subject that if he comes out, he will not be
harmed. For his part, the subject is confronted
with an array of heavily armed, helmeted, and flack-
jacketed police.

This specter causes the subject to face the prospect of his own vulnerability and imminent death.
The felon is rational enough to decide to survive.
The problem is to convince him that the awesome
array of force will not be used if he surrenders.
Many hostage negotiations eventually amount to this
type of persuasion by the police and a quest for
good faith and security by the subject. One nation-
ally prominent hostage negotiator told me that most
of what he does is to convince felons that if they
comeout and surrender, they will not be harmed.
Since this accounts for the largest portion of police experience with hostage negotiation, it is
easy to see why in the case of men who serve as
negotiators on a special weapons unit, negotiating
skills can further be deemphasized. After all, the
primary advantage to the negotiator appears to come
from the efficient deployment of a heavily armed
tactical weapons unit. Negotiation begins with a
subject who for all practical purposes is himself
a hostage, having been contained by the special
weapons unit. The appearance of this unit and the
efficiency with which it deploys itself are undoubtedly instrumental ingredients in the pressure
being applied to the subject. Thus, it is possible
for an individual who is part of the unit responsible for these activites to further emphasize in
his own mind the importance of the unit's tactics,
as opposed to the strategy of negotiation.

To some highly placed police officials, hostage
negotiation is not even perceived as demanding a

special set of skills. One high-ranking police
officer, who had gotten favorable publicity from
an episode that came out well despite some rather
questionable, if not inept, procedures, told me
that any police officer with experience understands
the criminal mind and that hostage-negotiating units
are unnecessary. During the episode in question, he
did not even attempt to draw upon the resources of
men in his own department who had formal training
and experience in negotiation procedures. While the
end result was a capitulation by the subjects and
a release of the hostages, it happened for reasons
that had little to do with good police procedure.
Unfortunately, success is perceived as its own val-
idation, and undoubtedly, future operations will
continue to be handled in a similar fashion until
such time as a major disaster results in some be-
lated introspection. In the meantime, the need for
a separate or even a trained negotiating unit will
continue to be viewed as unnecessary in this community.

TACTICAL PROCEDURES

     Where SWAT does not do the negotiating, its pri-
mary role is to maintain control of the inner perimeter. In any hostage or barricade situation, the
primary duty of the special weapons unit is to establish control of an inner perimeter. Generally,
the only police members in the inner perimeter are
members of SWAT and the negotiators. The watch-
words are "lock it in and stop the action." That
is SWAT's immediate function. The perpetrators
must be confined; the uniform patrol drops back to
establish an outer perimeter. Here, the crowd
control is established. Experience shows that the
longer the operation is in progress, the greater
the crowd. The uniformed patrol is not permitted
within the inner perimeter. Between the two perimeters, depending on local policy, members of the
press and public information officers are permitted.
The press is generally prohibited from the inner
perimeter, although some departments have taken the
position that if the press wants to take the risk,
they can go where the action is. Of course, the
pros and cons of such policies are debatable. All
civilians who are within the inner perimeter are,
if possible, evacuated. If not, they are warned
to stay inside and keep down, away from the windows.
     The inner perimeter is generally about a block

square, although some teams prefer, if possible,
a two-block-square area. Within the inner perimeter, an observation and command post are established, and communication lines to the perpetrators
are opened. The preference here has been for the
use of army field telephones. This is a result of
telephones being tied up by an overly eager press.
In some situations, the press has tied up phones to
such an extent that negotiators have had to request
that they relinquish the line in order for negotiations to begin. In New York, as a result of
press intrusion, special arrangements have been
made with the phone company to have all incoming
calls other than those initiated by the police phone
stopped and all outgoing calls ending up only at the
police phone. This procedure also prevents perpetrators from adopting dramatic forms of role behavior for publicity purposes.

As positions are assigned the special weapons
detail, the marksmen take up their position on the
site and also provide antisniper control. In San
Francisco, the marksmen are drawn from the district
and are supplemental to the special weapons team.

In all such situations, response time is a
vital ingredient. For this reason, in all departments, the special weapons units carry enough gear
in the trunks of their cars to respond to a call.
In Los Angeles, when officers are off duty two
members of each five man team are assigned equipped cars. The vehicles contain enough equipment
to sustain a responding team, pending the arrival
of the SWAT logistics truck. During normal working
hours, a 15-minute response time is considered av-
erage. There is an attempt to keep off duty response time within 30 minutes.

Intelligence gathering is initiated as the
team takes over from the uniformed patrol. It is
important to obtain descriptions of the perpetrators and the hostages, as well as their re-
spective numbers. If possible, the identities of
both parties should be established. This provides
information about the seriousness of the threat
and likely reactions of perpetrators and hostages.
Medical records are also vital if the use of gas is
likely. Knowledge of the location is important if
any assault or marksman action becomes likely. In
one hostage episode that I witnessed in the George-
town section of Washington, D.C., the location had
been completely remodeled, thus obviating the information available from the building plans. Fortunately, the interior designer, realizing that

knowledge of the interior layout might be vital
to the police, rushed to the scene with his render-
ings.

PROBLEMS FACING SWAT

The need for a SWAT-type operation in our major
metropolitan areas would appear to be accepted as
a vital part of police work. The concept of SWAT,
while of prime and visible political importance
during a dramatic hostage or barricade situation,
is unfortunately privy to little political support
at other times. SWAT does require extra resources
and specialized training, and this pulls men off
the street. Teams complain that when an operation
is in progress, politicians will sometimes violate
the security of the command post to gain on-the-
scene media exposure; yet, the same politicians are
often so restrained in their fiscal support of
the concept that some teams find it difficult to
obtain necessary equipment and even get enough
ammunition to keep up their proficiency in the use
of weapons. In a number of instances, the weapons
proficiency of SWAT operations has only been sustained by the sympathy and largess of National
Guard and Army commanders.

A SWAT commander also walks a public tightrope.
The operations he is frequently called upon to
handle are of strong press interest. They are
highly dramatic--they involve life and death decisions, are imbued with deeply stirring and vivid
emotions, and are played against a backdrop of
sirens, fast-moving cars, and men poised for dead-
ly action. The publicity rewards for a successful operation are virtually incalculable. But
publicity is based on result, not procedure. No
matter how professionally an operation is executed,
there is always the possibility that it will turn
out badly. As experienced police officers involved
in hostage negotiations have noted, there are principles and procedures that are applicable to hostage and barricade situations, and there are obviously some regularities in such situations, but
ultimately, each individual case is unique and,
consequently, unpredictable. One can do everything
by the book, follow all the rules and procedures,
make all the right guesses, and still there is that
crucial element of chance that one cannot control.
There is that idiosyncratic aspect of each case
and each subject that can turn a good operation

into a bad one. When that happens, it does not
make a difference how good the procedure was--
those in charge will, in the public eye, shoulder
the blame.

The converse, however, is also true. If an
operation is totally inept but the end result is
deemed successful, the press will be unrelenting
in its praise for the skills and competence of the
team. The unfortunate attribute of that outcome is
that the team gets so caught up in its own press
notices that it learns a little if anything of
what it should have learned from the operation.

In one such operation in a major metropolis,
noted in the press as an outstanding example of
police work, almost everything was done incorrectly.
According to procedures governing the use of the
SWAT team in the particular community, the district
commander was in charge of the operation. A good,
experienced officer who ran an efficient district,
he was without any special training in the tactics
of handling a hostage situation. Moreover, he felt
that experience overrode all and that specialized
training was neither vital nor necessary to the
conduct of the operation. The special weapons team
arrived on the scene to control the inner perimeter.
In a manner that would have shocked most tactical
units and sent a number of them packing their gear
and wanting no part of the operation, regular patrolmen and plainclothes detectives were assembled
within the inner perimeter with guns drawn. The
situation was anything but locked up and sealed.
When asked about controlling firepower, the commander responded by saying that he had such authority over his men that no one would have fired without his signal. That kind of confidence was mis-
placed, as some of his men went behind the building
and threw stones at the windows where the subjects
were holed up--in an attempt to get off a shot. This
took place while negotiations were in progress.

To add disaster to ludicrousness, the perpetrators demanded they name their own negotiators--
two well-known black members of the media. The
perpetrators, being black, did not trust dealing
with white policemen. The request was acceded to,
and all the major local television stations con-
verged on the scene to transmit the encounter. Network transmissions were aborted, as the unfolding
drama was carried live across the local airways.

After having been shot at earlier, the commander further acquiesced to the subjects' demands
to stand out in the street at gun range with the

two reporters and one of the subject's sisters, as
a show of good faith. One reporter, who demonstrated excellent judgment under pressure, refused.
The others responded to the request, and the perpetrators surrendered.

Fortunately, this operation, with its continual
violation of established procedure, ended well.
The media wanted heroes, and the reporters and the
district commander were vaulted into the limelight.
The two reporters informed me that the whole operation might have ended in disaster save for the per-
suasiveness of the subject's sister.

As things turned out, success embellished by
the media resulted in its own reconstruction and
creation of heroes. Both reporters actually wanted
little of it. It did not serve them well. Both
were prominent in their own right, and the additional media exposure, while useful to the station to
which one belonged, was not needed nor desired. As
for many of the police involved, the incident only
served to underscore a bad set of procedures that
had fortuitously, and despite the best attempts of
the police, worked out well.

SWAT AND THE MEDIA

It is always difficult to impute motivation in
an episode such as that just described; however,
one of the difficulties that both SWAT teams and
hostage negotiation teams commonly encounter is
the intrusion of politicians and high-ranking police officials seeking publicity. (What is ironic
about the preceeding situation is that it took
place in a community that had an exceptionally well-
trained special weapons team.) Some examples of
the disruptions that have taken place in operations
as a result of the encroachment of politicians or
higher-ranking officers seeking publicity are
presented.

In one example, a well-trained and highly
experienced negotiator wanted to go to face-to-
face negotiation after a long and measured encounter with the subject. The negotiator felt the
point had been reached where sufficient intimacy
and trust had been established and this procedure
was desirable. Although face-to-face negotiation
is common and this negotiator had done it many
times before, his superior, surrounded by the press,
adamantly refused to let him do it. The scene had
more to do with theater than a calculated command

decision.

In another example, a potential skyjacker
seized a private airplane at an airport in a large
metropolitan area. A command post was set up and
was soon overrun with the governor, the mayor, city
councilmen, and various and sundry of their associates. Eventually, there were so many politicians
and newsmen in the command post that the local SWAT
team and the FBI had to move the actual command
operation to the airfield.

In another example, a well-trained and well-led
SWAT team in a major city was instructed to put a
female on the team in deference to affirmative
action constraints. The team leader asked to be
able to select a female candidate from several of
the outstanding female officers in the force. He
was told whom to take. The female officer in question had never qualified for the team, although by
administrative fiat she was a member. She had
generated a lot of "good" press, which is exactly
what the officials wanted. At present, the team
was short one person, since the female member had
yet to qualify for any position. In my travels
from team to team around the country, there were
many questions about this particular female officer, who had been the subject of very favorable
but unrealistic press coverage. Unfortunately, for
both the team and those female officers who would
have qualified, police functions were placed in a
position subsidiary to the desire for publicity.

SWAT AS PUBLICITY AND FAD

Publicity, the idea of an elite unit, and the
dramatization of SWAT on TV have created other
problems for the concept. It appears that every
department throughout the country, irrespective
of size and need, has an application before the
International Association of Chiefs of Police to
have a SWAT team formed. Few have the need, budget,
talent, or training facilities to maintain such a
unit. But SWAT is popular, and it appears everyone is interested in cashing in on the fad. Such
quests appear to have the result of raising the
question as to whether or not SWAT is a necessary
concept anywhere.

The issue is easily resolved if one simply
considers the history of SWAT. In Los Angeles, the
concept developed out of the Watts riots of the
mid-1960s. There, police found that a talented

sniper with command of the terrain could tie up
an entire police force. Similar knowledge through
unfortunate experience was hammered home to the police throughout major metropolitan areas during
the riots of the mid-1960s. The mass demonstrations
of the same period forced the police to confront
the need to develop new tactics to deal with mass
confrontation, especially when mass demonstrations
escalated from nonviolence to violence or when
undisciplined police reactions produced the same
results as escalation would have.

In Washington, D.C., the SWAT unit grew out of
an ill-fated attempt by officers to respond to a
scene in February 1969 where a man had barricaded
himself with a shotgun. The first two responding
officers sustained injuries, as did their backup.
The department realized that a specialized set of
tactics was required for this and other extraordinary situations. From this emerged the concept of what D.C. police call the "barricade
squad."

One of the most dramatic incidents that high-
lighted the need for a SWAT-type operation occurred in New Orleans several years ago. A sniper
atop a tall building held the entire police force
at bay for several hours. Patrolmen with .38s
were observed attempting to hit the subject by
lobbing bullets up in the air. When police finally
rushed the subject, a number of officers were killed and injured from ricocheting police bullets unleashed in a fusillade of fire. The subject had
been dead hours before the assault took place.

With various forms of political terrorism on
the rise, internationally and domestically, there
is little doubt that SWAT-type units are vital and
necessary. The problem appears to be one of gaining proper public acceptance of the concept and
public support for its funding. SWAT teams are
not vital to the police program of every city.
Under mutual aid and assistance agreements, the
services of such units can be obtained from neighboring metropolises or, in the case of violation
of federal law, from the FBI. In the negotiation
for hostages, the SWAT operation not only provides
vital tactical support but important psychological
impact as well. After all, hostage negotiation
techniques are an extension of normal police tactics
not a substitute for them.

APPENDIX: TACTICAL PROCEDURES--BASIC ELEMENTS

The existence of a special weapons team man-
dates a set of tactical procedures to be executed
under emergency conditions. Although tactical
procedures will have to accomodate circumstances
and environments, it is important that certain
predetermined guidelines be established. This is
not to limit flexibility but to set out a series
of functional responses that will most likely be
applicable under a wide variety of circumstances.

The initiation of any procedure requires basic
information as to what is happening at the scene.
The first order of business for the tactical unit
is to secure information from the uniform patrol.
Such information would include:

1.   Where is the action taking place?
2.   Who is involved (description and number)?
3.   What weapons do the subjects have?
4.   Why are the subjects engaged in this
     activity?
5.   What has happened thus far? Has there
     been any shooting? Are there any in-
     juries, casualties, or hostages taken,
     and so forth?

Obtaining such information is vital to the function of creating an inner perimeter. Before the
scene can be locked up and closed off, the men who
are about to undertake that function must know
what they are confronting. Even the size of the
perimeter itself and the ability to exercise lat-
eral and vertical advantage will be contingent on
the disposition of information obtained. Moreover, it is imperative that the team establishing
and maintaining the inner perimeter be protected
from potential snipers or a hostile populace. Consequently, suitable positions will have to be established to provide covering fire on all sides.
The establishment of these positions is also contingent on knowledge obtained concerning the disposition of the scene.

The establishment of the inner perimeter brings
access to the scene under restriction, prevents the
movement of the subjects from the scene, removes
civilian personnel from potentially dangerous exposure, and stops the action so that necessary intelligence gathering can continue and a tactical

plan can be devised.

As the tactical unit is establishing the inner perimeter, the uniformed patrol falls back to establish an outer perimeter. This perimeter functions to (1) restrict the access of all traffic and pedestrians that might come into potential conflict with the police in the performance of their duties, (2) establish the external boundaries of an evacuation area to protect civilians from possible gunfire, and (3) establish between the boundaries of the two perimeters an area for the dissemination of information to authorized members of the media.

Between the two perimeters is the tactical command post, or TCP. The TCP functions to direct the special weapons operation within the inner perimeter. In small operations, the TCP may also serve as the main or overall command post; however, in large operations, the TCP's control is limited to the tactical command, with an overall operational command maintained separately and under the direction of higher-level police personnel.

The operational command post, or OCP, has operational control over the entire operation and has final jurisdictional authority. However, once an order is given to the TCP, it is up to the tactical leader to decide how and when the order will be implemented. The OCP is responsible for the total decision, supervision, and decision making. As the command decision is its primary function, support functions are maintained through subsidiary sections, which are staffed by appointments made to the commander. These functions include but are not limited to the following:

1. Operations--this section is responsible for overall coordination of information and maintenance of pertinent records and data. Decisions and directions for the overall operation are transmitted from this section.
2. Logistics and communications--this section is responsible for providing logistics support in the form of equipment and manpower and in establishing and maintaining communications equipment. This section is also responsible for securing additional special weapons teams.
3. Intelligence and investigations--this section handles the gathering of pertinent intelligence data and investigates the situation at the crime scene. The dis-

semination and processing of intelligence
data is only undertaken by this section
upon clearance and direction from the operations unit.
4. Liaison--this unit is responsible for maintaining liaison with the news media. It
conducts, under the direction of, and from
information supplied by, the operations
section, news conferences, and briefings.
It also maintains and restricts the area to
which the press has access. It directs the
press to preestablished locations for major
announcements and is responsible for coordinating efforts to keep the press out of
the inner perimeter.

The structure and procedures outlined here are
only one reconstruction of a mode of operation.
Each situation and the basic policies of each police
department will mandate their own procdures. There
are, however, certain elements in the above procedures that would be useful under almost any circumstances and should most likely be incorporated
in any set of operational and tactical considerations. These principles include the following:

1. Containment of the situation and the restriction of access should be the primary objective.
2. The special weapons unit should be completely and solely in control of, and responsible for,
the security of the inner perimeter. This enables
the maintenance of discipline and the control of
firepower.
3. The tactical and operational command posts
should be physically and hierarchically separated
in a serious situation.
4. Ultimate authority and decision making
resides with the OCP. However, the TCP must re-
tain discretionary decision making as to how to
implement the operational commander's decisions.
5. A division of labor should be maintained
between the two commands. This centralizes authority in a single location and yet permits the
discretionary authority appropriate to a commander
with specialized knowledge and skills.
6. There should be a distinct means of providing for the centralization of operations, logistics, and communications functions, intelligence
and investigative roles, and for liaison with the
press. These functions should be executed under
the supervision of the commanding officer but con-

ducted in such a fashion that they do not interfere
with the imperative of command decisions. The
centralization of these functions means that incoming and outgoing information is regulated and
disseminated through a single communications location. This tends to ensure that everyone has
the same information.

7. Establishing the liaison section is imperative. This prevents the adverse affects that can
result from the circulation of rumors. Liaison
work, while directed at the community through the
press, must at times result in communication directly with the community to defuse rumors that
would turn a barricade situation into a riot.

These elements, then, appear to be essential
ingredients of any operation, and mechanisms that
incorporate them will of course tend to vary. The
mechanism used for incorporation is less important
than the fact that the function has been performed.

5
Terrorism and the Media: A Dilemma

INTRODUCTION

Mark Twain, the American humorist, once said, "The American people enjoy three great blessings: free speech, free press, and a good sense not to use either." We confront the problem of terrorism and the media because we have not paid proper deference to Twain's engaging cynicism. We have exercised our freedom of the press, and we have sometimes done so in a fashion that did not demonstrate the exercise of good sense.

The issue of the media and terrorism is a complex one. It raises thorny problems that pit concerns for first amendment freedoms and concerns with the invaluable role of the press in a democratic society against humanitarian concerns for saving lives. This is not an abstract conflict. It continually manifests itself in real-life situations where human life is imminently at stake. The problem promotes neither easy answeres nor complex solutions but rather complex choices. The exercise of any one of these choices will leave some constituency dissatisfied.

Much of terrorism is undertaken solely for dramatic effect. Brian Jenkins,[1] of RAND Corporation, has prominently argued this position. Baljit Singh,[2] of Michigan State University, has amplified this idea, noting that the publicity terrorists seek is also a means of getting access to the public agenda. It is an attempt to have their grievances discussed within the international community. Many terrorist episodes appear to have no other function than that of getting publicity. The September 1976 hijacking of a Trans World Airlines flight by Croatian separatists is a case in point. Not only were the terrorists unarmed and with no hope of obtaining sanctuary, but their demands were directed at obtaining publicity. Prior to the terrorist episode, who but a few authorities on Europe ever heard of Croatia? Similarly, the terrifying actions of the Hanafi Muslims who held Washington, D.C., at bay in March of 1977, were, when fully understood, little more than an attempt to obtain media exposure.[3] Hamass Abdul Khaalis, the Hanafi leader, upon surrender, admitted to police that he never anticipated that the authorities would give in to his demands.

What did Khaalis obtain for his efforts? Media exposure, in otherwise unreachable proportions. There was continuous live television coverage; domination of virtually the entire first section of the Washington Post for two days; and transatlantic phone interviews. The event transformed the Hanafi Muslims from a little-known group, even within Washington, to the focal point of national and international media coverage.

In executing the dramaturgy written for presentation in Washington, Khaalis had taken a leaf from Abane Ramdane, a leader of the Algerian resistance, who is responsible for having moved Algerian guerilla warfare from the countryside to the city. His decision to change tactics was based on the observation that the act of killing ten French people in the desert went unnoticed while the killing of one French person on a busy street in Algiers would receive coverage in the international media.[4] The literature on terrorism has inappropriately portrayed Latin America as the arena for the transition of guerrilla warfare from a rural to an urban phenomenon.[5] The change took place much earlier, in the Algerian conflict, and because of the desire for access to the media.

Abane Ramdane has bequeathed a legacy to Dr. George Habash of the Popular Front for the Liberation of Palestine. Habash, the father of airplane hijacking for political exposure, has argued that killing a single Jew and getting publicity is more important than killing scores of Jews in a battle. As he has noted, "When we set fire to a store in London (referring to the incendiary bombs in Marks and Spencer, August 17, 1969), those few flames are worth the burning down of two Kibbutzim (Israeli agricultural settlements) because we force people to ask what is going on...."[6]

Inasmuch as terrorism seeks access to the public agenda, it is dependent on the media. One might hesitatingly say it is the media's step-

child. This is not to lapse into the ancient cus-
tom of condemning the messenger for bringing dis-
tressing news nor is it to blame the media for terrorism. After all, modern terrorism is based on a
rather vulgar interpretation of Karl Marx's notion
that revolutions come about with the increasing
immiseration of society. Terrorists seek to create
a climate of fear and insecurity resulting in a
lack of confidence in the government and a demand
for the government to exercise harsher methods and
a stronger resolve in combating terrorism. The
implementation of such methods is perceived as
leading to a harsher, more authoritarian, and capricious exercise of power, leading to greater immiseration and an ensuing mass uprising. More
likely, of course, the terrorist actions when leading to more restrictive measures are most likely
going to lead to a right-wing coup that will simultaneously remove the terrorists, the government,
and whatever additional opposition exists. Such
was the case in Uruguay. The army overthrew the
government and decimated the Tupamaros.
     It is immaterial whether this scenario of rev-
olution has any prospect of working. The terrorists believe that it works, and consequently they
act on that belief. Its implementation requires
the creation of a climate of fear. That climate
can only be brought about by using the media. A
terrorist action that does not attract media coverage can hardly contribute to the climate of fear.
Terrorism demands media coverage in order to a-
chieve its required impact. As Brian Jenkins noted, "Terrorists want a lot of people watching and
a lot of people listening.... Terrorists choreograph
incidents to achieve maximum publicity, and in
that sense, terrorism is theater."[7]
     With this desire for exposure has come the re-
liance on the spectacular event, an event that pre-
sents a good visual drama. Correspondent Neil
Hickey has observed that "many terrorist incidents
that are covered routinely in the back pages of
newspapers get prominent treatment in TV news
broadcast because of their visual drama and excitement."[8]
     The medium is so essential to the drama that
during the OPEC kidnappings in Vienna, the notori-
ous Carlos, the leader of the operation, stayed in
the headquarters building until the television cameras arrived. The posturing for coverage reminded
one of Columbia University Professor J. Bowyer
Bell's quips describing the sometime symbionic re-

lationship between terrorism and the media, "Don't shoot, Abdul! We're not on prime time!"[9]

ACKNOWLEDGING THE PROBLEM

Until recently, few media people concerned themselves with the problem. One noteworthy exception is Stephen Rosenfeld, of the Washington Post, who wrote the following before it was fashionable to do so: "We of the Western Press have yet to come to terms with international terror. If we thought about it more and understood its essence, we would probably stop writing about it, or we would write about it with a great deal of restraint."[10]

Rosenfeld's sensitive observations were shared by one West German TV editor who spoke with Melvin J. Lasky about the events surrounding the kidnapping of West Berlin mayoral candidate Peter Lorenz. "For 72 hours we just lost control of the medium, it was theirs, not ours...We shifted shows in order to meet their timetable. Our cameras had to be in position to record each of the released prisoners as they boarded the plane to freedom, and our news coverage had to include prepared statements of their dictate...It's never happened before...Surely it must be the first recorded case of how to hijack a TV network!..."[11]

In this preceding episode, we are noting the forced compliance of the media with terrorist demands, a compliance that ensued as part of the deal made for the release of Peter Lorenz. Here, the media had little choice. The episode demonstrates that even where the primary demands of the terrorists are achieved, the secondary demands for media exposure are not rescinded. That in itself is a profound commentary on the importance of media exposure to terrorist activity.

CONSTRAINTS ON SOLUTION

Would we have terrorism if there were no media? Certainly, but probably less and of a different variety. We cannot, however, ignore reality. The media does exist, and its job is to report the news. Terrorist attacks are news. In a competitive news industry, what one source fails to report others will seize. It would be impractical for the media to ignore terrorist events. And even if it

were not, the withholding of this kind of information from the public would ultimately have some
negative and unanticipated consequences. Utimate-
ly, the terrorists would increase the scope of
their activities or select such prominent targets
that the media could no longer afford to ignore
them.

THE PROBLEMS OF MEDIA INTRUSION AND MEDIA DEPICTION

The reporting of events is not the prime issue.
We are more concerned with how these events are
reported, and equally important, we are concerned
with the role that reporters play in some of these
episodes. These are related but somehow separate
issues. The latter issue is one that has raised
the ire of our police, and in many cases, justifiably so. Reporters have intruded on the police
in the performance of their duties. The actions of
overzealous reporters have directly put lives in
jeopardy. On a day-to-day basis, men such as Assistant Chief Robert Rabe, head negotiator for the
Washington, D.C., police, have had to face that
kind of intrusion. His eloquent statements concerning the problem merits attention.[12]
It has been commonplace for members of the
media to argue that they cannot report the news unless they can get access to the news. This had
meant access to the place where the action is
taking place. Courts have upheld this right, and
police departments have incorporated procedures to
provide for access with appropriate concern for the
security and the safety of the press as well as the
need for the police to be unimpeded in their work.
Terrorist episodes, especially hostage situations, are made of the stuff that sells copy. They
are dramatic and violent, and life hangs in the
balance. The pendulum of decision making swings
back and forth: demand, counterdemand, give and
take. There is the human interest element, the
anxiety-ridden relatives waiting for fate to make
its move. Whose loved ones will survive and whose
will perish? In such situations there is pressure
for a scoop, for some new angle, for an exclusive
interview with the perpetrators. The journalistic
rewards are great, and these sometimes take prece-
dence over common sense and concern for the life
and welfare of the victims.
These pressures lead to actions by the media
that have directly impaired police operations.

Such actions are all too common. And both the
police and the press are aware of their existence.
In my travels around this country interviewing
police negotiating teams, almost every team had
experienced some episode where an overzealous press
had jeopardized an operation. These actions have
varied from reporters tying up the phone lines,
making it impossible for negotiations to begin, to
broadcasting details of police procedure and thus
providing the perpetrators with useful tactical
knowledge. The media has served as the eyes and
ears of terrorists and has inadvertently assisted
them during the execution of operations.

If these charges sound incredible, perhaps some
details may be of value here. In New York City,
the hostage negotiation team had talked a perpetrator into surrendering. As he approached the
door, the phone rang. It was a reporter. He
wanted to know why the perpetrator got involved,
and the perpetrator's grievances were rekindled.
He got back into his role, and it took the police
another three hours to talk him out. In the 1974
hostage episode at the District of Columbia Courthouse, a two-way mirror separated the hostages and
their captors from the police, providing the police with complete knowledge of the situation and
the option of using snipers if the lives of the
hostages came into jeopardy. Unfortunately, the
media broadcasted that piece of information, and
the hostages were quickly dispatched to taping
newspaper over the glass. In the Hanafi Muslim
episode, when the police began to bring contain-
ers of food toward the building, the press broadcasted the undertaking as preparation for an imminent assault. Had the police not been able to
convince the Hanafis that the broadcast was in-
correct, gunfire would have erupted.

On too many occasions the media have held live
interviews over the airways with terrorists holding
hostages. Anyone remotely acquainted with the
tensions and pressures that build up in hostage
situations knows how fragile these situations are.
A slip of the tongue, a poorly chosen phrase, or
an intonation that rings of dissonance can have
tragic consequences. Police negotiators are given
hours of intensive training, learning how to engage
suspects in conversation, what things to pursue and
what things not to pursue. They work with backup
units that monitor the conversation and exercise
guidance and direction, signaling the negotiator to
go forward with or back off from a topic. The ne-

gotiation is so delicate that it cannot be left to
one person. And there have been times when an experienced negotiator cannot build rapport with a
suspect and the original negotiator has to be replaced.

The intervention of an untrained journalist in
this process is simply playing games with people's
lives. Aside from the lack of training, a journalist is first and foremost a journalist. He or
she is looking for a story. The journalist's mind
set is directed at getting the best story possible.
Any interview with a terrorist holding lives in
the balance has some prospect of jeopardizing those
lives, but when the interview is also live, the
situation brings together the composite pressures
of being on the air with the gnawing knowledge that
the person at the other end of the phone is armed,
dangerous, and threatening to kill. Is the public's right to know worth more that the lives of
the hostages, especially when it is not a question
of the public knowing or not knowing but of how
long they will have to wait for information? Such
live interviews have far and away more to do with
sensationalism and ratings than with any philosophical concern for the value of public information in a democratic society. They tend to provide less in the way of useful information than to
serve as an unobtrusive commentary on the insensi-
tivity of the press to the safety and well-being of
victims.

Beyond this, there is the issue of journalists
acting as negotiators when they have been called
upon to do so by civil authorities. I would, except in the most unique situations, question the
wisdom of such decisions. When called upon by
authorities to perform in this capacity, a journalist does not face an easy nor a necessarily re-
warding task. Such a journalist starts out with
the additional handicap of having his or her presence in that role signify that the police were unable to fulfill their obligation to the community.
The police may have requested the journalist's
presence, but to some extent they will resent the
journalist's being there. The circumstances that
necessitated the presence are simultaneously reflective of their failure. If the situation does
end badly, the journalist bears the potential af-
flication of being a public scapegoat, not to men-
tion the burden of his or her own guilt.

Once such a request is made of a journalist, it
is not readily turned down. To refuse will not

only evoke a disfavorable response from one's employer but would be viewed in the larger community as a disavowal of one's social responsibility, a designation no one in the public eye can afford.

• I have interviewed journalists who were cast into the role of hostage negotiators when captors refused to deal with the police. One of these journalists, a particularly insightful and sensitive individual, a person whose work had won several commendations, resented the role. He said that the emotional strain was incredible. He was unprepared for it. He shuddered at the thought of life and death hanging in the balance. He had no frame of reference against which to interpret what was happening. The police were of little help. They resented his presence, and they had become caught up in the media apsects of the event. They wanted to bask in the flood of television lights. The desire by the police for media attention was so great that the professional team was relegated to containing an outer perimeter while the local commander personally took charge. The police who were in charge were no better prepared to deal with the tactical or psychological requirements of the situation than the journalist was. The police who were experienced, trained, and capable had been diverted to supporting duties. Fortunately, despite it all, it ended well. The journalist said he would never do it again. It was a law-enforcement operation, and his presence signified that the law-enforcement people had not established enough trust in the community to do their job.

The journalist became front-page news. Over fifty media sources had requested interviews. His employer promoted it, saw it as good for public relations and, of course, income. The journalist reluctantly continued to play the role of hero. He had candidly confessed to me that he had no use for the role or the exposure. His objectivity in analyzing the situation, however, was unfazed by his emerging as a hero. The outcome had turned on luck, he confided, not skill.

This kind of sensitivity is as rare as it is refreshing. Unfortunately, all too often another kind of response emerged. Too many media people were willing to chance other people's lives and sometimes their own for a chance at success. One reporter who had actively been involved in a long hostage situation, told me, when asked about any fear he had about inadvertently angering the captors during the course of the interviews he conducted: "I never thought about getting them riled up. My primary goal was to be let into...and to get a scoop. My gratification comes from doing something that is worthy of the front page...doing a story worth seeing. Probably, there in the back of my mind there was concern, but I didn't think about it."

I do not want to portray media people as being insensitive to concerns for human life. It is, however, important that we recognize the real pressures that media people, when thrust into a terrorist situation, even when limiting themselves to their professional role, must experience. It is for this reason that legitimate concerns for human life must be exercised to limit sharply the role of the media personnel as either warranted or unwarranted negotiators.

There is another question concerning the media's role that deserves equal attention. This is the issue of how the media portrays terrorist episodes. To my knowledge, there have been no systematic studies of this problem. Professor Robert Jackson and associates have recently completed some work on collective conflict and the Canadian media. As their study did not deal with terrorism per se, it is difficult to make any confident inferences from their findings. However, it may be worth noting that among their findings were the following:

There is a tendency in the media to focus overwhelmingly on violence, while obscuring the issue of confrontation.

There are indications that media presence at the scene of a disturbance has on occasion stimulated confrontation.

It is evident that the media on occasion became involved in the creation of news, either by consciously allowing themselves to be manipulated by dramatic protesters or by directly orchestrating an event...[13]

It is the latter finding that should concern us most, for it is apparent that the dramatic personalities on the terrorist stage have also milked the media.

In this vein, Louis Rukeyser has noted about the American news coverage of Arab terrorists:

American news coverage of the Arab guerrillas
in recent years has resembled nothing so much as
American news coverage of the Black Panthers--
and in neither case has my profession covered
itself with journalistic glory. With both
groups there is fascination with the reality and
threat of violence. With both there was a tendency to overrate their influence and to take
with grave seriousness the most nonsensical extremes of rhetoric.
In the case of the guerrillas, this resulted in
some rather extensive news coverage aimed at
perpetrating the notion that these militants now
had the central role in determining the future
of the Middle East. In fact, this has never
been true as has increasingly become clear.
In my own travels in the area, including visits
to nearly all the countries even remotely involved, I became convinced early on that the war
in the Middle East would remain inevitable as
long as two basic conditions continued--first,
an Arab unwillingness genuinely to accept the
permanence of Israel and second, a determination
by the Soviet Union to egg the Arabs on and supply them with necessary armaments. All else is
secondary. The guerrillas, far from being the
dominant force in the region, in reality have
been shut off and turned on like a propaganda
spigot by the Arab governments that border Israel.... Mideast peace depends more than ever not
on the hot oratory of a colorful, guerrilla but
on the cold decisions of the Kremlin.[14]

Similarly, John Lafflin has noted that the
"Fedayeen have had extraordinarily good publicity in
the West--better than that given to Israel--being
presented pretty much on their own terms as heroes
and resistance fighters on the classical anti-Nazism
pattern, a gallant few facing fearful odds. They
were romaticized by the media in the U.S., Britain,
and much of Europe to appear as idealistic daredevils
and diehards."[15]
These are impressions, of course, and all of us
may not share them. They should at least motivate
us to give some thoughtful consideration to whether
or not the media is manipulated by the drama of an
event or the charisma of a terrorist leader to the
point where excitement feeds fantasy and objective
reporting loses to the art of dramaturgy. In this
regard, I recall the appearance of Yassir Arafat before the United Nations. In viewing the deference

accorded him and his portrayal by the mass media, I
could have become convinced of the efficacy of terrorism. It appeared that terrorism does work, and
Arafat's appearance before the United Nations was
living proof. Terrorism also appeared to create
statesmen--albeit those who carry guns to diplomatic
gatherings. I could have been convinced, but I was
not--because I recalled two things the media seemed
to ignore. One was that no other guerrilla leader
had been received in this fashion, prior to a-
chieving victory, and the other was the price and
scarcity of oil. Somehow, what was ignored seemed
to speak far and away more decisively that what was
said.

It is somewhat unfortunate that much of what has
been noted previously is critical of the media, I do
not wish to appear to portray a solely negative image of the vital role of the media. As the media
ignores the commonplace and normal functioning of
society, we ignore the commonplace and enormously
important functions of the media. After all, those
aspects do not present problems. Moreover, there is
basic agreement about the importance of a free and
unobstructed media. The police do not advocate government intrusion into the operations of the media.
They have asked that the media exercise responsible
judgment, that the media become aware of the dependence of many forms of terrorist activity on the
media, and that reporters in their zeal to pursue a
story, in the exercise of their constitutionally
sanctioned freedoms, remember that their right to a
story is not as important as a victim's right to
survive.

We are painfully aware that the press has heard
similar concepts before. The admonition to exercise
self-restraint was heard throughout Vietnam and
later during Watergate. If the press had acquiesced
to such appeals, the truth would have taken even
longer to emerge, if it would have emerged at all.
Because the freedom of the press is so important, we
should be concerned that is abuse could ultimately
lead to public clamor for government intrusion.
Freedom of the press is too important a right to be
left to government control. At the same time, the
right of a hostage to survive and the right of a
society to self-preservations are also important
rights, too important to be left to the media. That
is the conflict that has brought the press, law-
enforcement, and the academic communities together,
in mutual distrust, admittedly, but in mutual concern
as well. It is, perhaps, recognition of that mutual

concern that will help pave the road to reasonable accomodation, if not to solution.

REFERENCES

1. Brian Jenkins, remarks to the Conference on International Political Terrorism, Evian, France, June 1977.

2. Baljit Singh, statements made to the XVII Annual Convention of the International Studies Association, March 16, 1977, St. Louis, Missouri. See also his Political Terrorism: Some Third World Perspectives (unpublished).

3. For an in-depth discussion of the Hanafi Muslim episode see Abraham H. Miller, "Negotiations for Hostages: Implications from the Police Experience," Terrorism: An International Journal, vol. 1 no. 2, 1978.

4. Roland Gauches, Les Terrorists (Paris: Editions Albin Michel, 1965), p. 262.

5. Thomas G. Clines, The Urban Insurgents, (Newport, Rhode Island: Naval War College, 1972).

6. George Habash to Oriana Fallaci, Life, June 22, 1970.

7. Jenkins quoted to Neil Hickey, "Terrorism and Television," T.V. Guide, July 31-August 6, 1977.

8. Ibid., p. 6.

9. From personal conversation.

10. Stephen S. Rosenfeld, Washington Post, November 21, 1975.

11. Melvin J. Lasky, "Ulrike Meinhof and the Baader-Meinhof Gang," Encounter 44 (June 1975) pp. 15-16.

12. Robert L. Rabe, "Terrorism and the Media: An Issue of Responsible Journalism," Terrorism, 2, Numbers 1 & 2, 1979, pp. 67-79.

13. Robert J. Jackson, Michael J. Kelly, and Thomas H. Mitchell, "Collective Conflict, Violence, and the Media in Canada," (Ottawa: Carleton University, unpublished).

14. Louis Rukeyser, American Information Radio Network, March 14, 1972.

15. John Lafflin, Fedayeen, (Glencoe: The Free Press, 1973), p. 113.

6
Terrorism and Government Policy

INTRODUCTION

Terrorism is technology's stepchild, an off-
spring of the dependence of modern society on complex networks of technology, the accessibility of
sophisticated weaponry,and a compliant mass media.
In the ranking of the severity of political violence, terrorism is preceded by guerrilla warfare
and even civil disorder. Unlike those expressions,
it is conducive to small numbers, requires few resources, and is more politically significant is appearance than in reality. It is the political tool
of the weak, of those whose political movements are
so embryonic that access to the public agenda is a
sufficient motivation for bloodshed. It thrives
primarily, although certainly not exclusively, on
random violence. This form of violence is insidi-
ous in its contamination of society through a fear
and insecurity that marks everyone as a potential
target. Random violence destroys the delusion of
escape into noninvolvement. The stark, harrowing,
and unavoidable message of terrorism is that no one
is safe, all are potential victims.[1]
Terrorism is best understood, perhaps only
properly understood, in its relationship to political violence generally. It is in the context of
this understanding that the role and value of the
terrorist's message and the media as its transmit-
ter becomes fully comprehensible. The crux of political violence, in all its forms, is the same as
that of politics generally. To paraphrase Harold
D. Lasswell, it is who gets what, when, and how.[2]
Because of this failure to see terrorism in the
larger context of political violence, we often lose
sight of the fact that terrorism is not so much an
end in itself as a means to an end; that end being

political power. Terrorism, in and of itself, has
not toppled governments. When used as a tactic in
conjunction with guerrilla warfare, it has hastened
the departure of some colonial regimes, as in Mandate Palestine, Cyprus, and Algeria, to name but a
few. But terrorism as a strategy is only the embryonic stage of a political movement which must
grow, strengthen, and mature into a full-blown mass
social and political movement in order to effectively topple regimes.

Ted Robert Gurr[3] has proposed an intriguing
conceptual device for assessing the various modes
of political violence. Seeing political conflict
in the Lasswellian sense, as a struggle between
those who have power and those who want to take it,
Gurr notes that the type of violent conflict which
eventually ensues is dependent on the relative balance of power between the opposing forces. Consequently, when the balance between opposing forces
is nearly equal, the mode of expression for that
conflict is civil war. When those out of power
have more strength than those in power, the result
is coup d'etat. When the reverse is true--those in
power have the balance heavily tilted in their fa-
vor--the result is riots and civil disorder. Although Gurr does not deal explicitly with terrorism, the logic of his presentation would lead one
to conclude that as a strategy (an expression of
political violence and not a tactic)terrorism must
precede riots and civil disorder, for the latter are
more potent forms of political violence and require
a mass base.

A continuum running the gamut of political violence from terrorism to civil war to coup d'etat
illustrates that while the ultimate goal of terrorism is to gain access to the corridors of power,
terrorists by and large are ill equipped to achieve
that goal. The greater the ability of a group to
achieve its ultimate goal, the less likely it will
choose terrorism as a mode of operation. When a
group primarily directs its activity toward terrorism, such action indicates how actually limited
are its resources. The resource base of terrorist
groups is generally so limited that the group may
be largely seeking publicity through the propaganda of the deed. And it is here that the concern
with random violence, in the contemporary form of
terrorism, is especially significant.

Random violence provides spectacular media
copy. Terrorism is frequently a combination of
brutality and violence mixed with a twist of irony.

Consider the spectacle of the blood-drenched Lod
Airport terminal (May 1972), made all the more incredible by the realization that members of the Japanese Red Army had indiscriminately slaughtered
Puerto Ricans,on a Christian pilgrimage,in order to
bring about the creation of a homeland for Palestinians. It is theatre which captures our attention,
but the theatre of the absurd played against spectacular violence becomes a media event seized with
a vengeance.

When terrorist episodes run in close proximity
to each other and are devoured by a media hungry
for spectacle, the impact on the public conscious-
ness is awesome. At such moments, the threat transcends geographic frontiers and even the most re-
mote spectators of the drama must confront their
own vulnerabilities. In these moments, the reality
of terrorism makes itself known, immediately and
unavoidably. A high-ranking New York Police Department officer, for example, is riveted to the TV
screen as the drama of the Munich Olympiad unfolds
and is angered by the tactical blunders committed
by the West German Police. In the days that follow, he is haunted by the question of how the New
York police would respond to a similar situation
and concludes that he does not want to engage the
answer. The event of Munich and the existence of a
large and prominent diplomatic community in New York
prompt the officer to develop a special unit to deal
with the tactical imperatives of hostage situations.[4]

The necessity of recognizing terrorism as an
immediate or potential problem is inescapable at
such moments. Eventually, inevitably, however, in
this country at least, when such crises pass and
the media turns to the next drama to be pandered to
mass culture, when the government crisis observers
and managers return to their daily bureaucratic
routines, and when the special police units have
put away their auxiliary weapons, the public and the
government appear to forget, if not to ignore. Life
and policy concerns return to routine.[5]

In regard to the development of effective policy
to deal with terrorism, Senator Jacob K. Javits
(New York) has noted, "I am becoming increasingly
apprehensive that the Carter administration has relinquished the lead expected of the United States
in this struggle by the rest of the civilized
world."[6] Senator Javits goes on to note that the
administration's initiative in this area has consisted of little more than a reshuffling of the al-

ready existing bureaucracy established in 1972 to
deal with terrorism, and that the State Department's
Office for Combating Terrorism, already highly
criticized as being inadequate in terms of authority, intelligence, and operational capabilities,
has been delegated no new authority and remains
functionally inadequate.[7]

Effective policy to deal with terrorism has
been lacking in the United States because terrorism
is not seem as a serious threat to governmental
stability. Consequently, in the aftermath of terrorist incidents, in ostensible homage to dispas-
sion, and in an attempt to put terrorism in perspective, government analysts have emerged to poke
at, dissect, translate, and explain the "true" significance of what transpired. The analysts are not
always in agreement, but recently there appears to
have emerged a repeated theme. It is one that has
achieved significance by force of repetition and
because it espouses a point of view that the Carter
administration wants to hear: "terrorism is not a
significant threat, at least not in so far as this
country is concerned."

If the meaning of this message is too easily
lost, it is buttressed by a number of pithy statements, often summarizing some excrutiatingly-culled
statistical data designed to make the point, e.g.
"The total cost of transnational terrorism, worldwide, in any one year is less than the cost of
crime in any midsized American city. An American
businessman abroad is less likely to be killed by
terrorists than he is likely to be killed by dog
bite. Terrorism is the newest growth industry,
overrun with self-proclaimed experts who are predisposed to overdraw the problem so as to drama-
tize their own importance."

As far as they go, statements like these are
not totally inaccurate. They are, however, quite
incomplete and myopic. Such myopia not only shapes
perceptionsof terrorism as it currently functions
but also of any reasonable prognosis of future acts
of terrorism. Putting the matter into focus, however, is not as readily accomplished as might be
desired. To begin with, it is necessary to counter
a number of pieces of statistical information whose
accuracy is indisputable but the interpretation of
which leaves something to be desired.

The succinct and loaded statements are based on
several rather questionable assumptions: (1) the
only important assessment of terrorism is a quantitative one which can measure the direct cost of

terrorism in terms of property, lives and injuries;
(2) the United States need not concern itself with
the operations or effects of international terrorism or even view it as having any relevance for the
development of domestic terrorism; (3) future acts
of terrorism as they affect the domestic concerns
of the United States can be summed up as looking
very much like the present, only more so. (This
type of prediction is one that those nurtured on
the linear models of modern social science take as
equivalent to natural law.)

It has become fashionable to the point of chic
in government and academic circles to assess virtually any problem through some quantitative for-
mula (remember those body counts in Vietnam). Such
assessments follow a law of the instrument--only
what is translatable into numbers is important, all
else is insignificant. Qualitative aspects of a
problem must be ignored or set aside as irrelevant.
Take, for example, what a quantitative assessment
of Black September's action at the 1972 Munich Olympiad, granted this mind-set, would look like. One
would inquire as to the obvious fatality count. To
this could be added some reasonable assessment of
the cost to the West German Government to execute
the operation, maintain crowd control,and direct
traffic. At some point all of this could be trans-
lated into a quantitative commodity. This in turn
could engender some pithy statement to the effect
that: "The total impact of the terrorist operation
at Munich was less significant in dollar cost and
lives lost than the results from one day's traf-
ficking in heroin in any large American city (pick
your own). Ergo, reasonable, knowledgeable,and
informed people would appreciate the true insignif-
icance of the events at Munich."

CONTROLLING THE PUBLIC AGENDA

Such depictions, of course, inexorably violate
our common sense. They refuse to engage even remotely the symbolic aspects of a political event.
They implicitly ignore one of the most common attributes of political terrorism--the target is usually not the immediate victim but a larger audience
capable of shaping the climate of public opinion.
Terrorism is concerned with having a psychological
impact as well as demanding access to the public
forum. Such factors are so critical that they determine how and where terrorists strike. No mean-

ingful assessment of terrorism can ignore these aspects.

But the quantitative assessments, concerned with pigeonholing information into preformed compartments, bypass the larger aspects of terrorism. The importance of access to the public agenda, as well as the opportunity to rewrite and even curtail it, are not so readily measured as are casualties and operations costs. The Black September operation at the Munich Olympiad was a theatre event that garnered maximum publicity for the Palestinian cause. In that sense, it put the Palestinian cause on the public agenda. However, there was, at least in the eyes of some observers, more to it than that. The operation was not only a theatre event designed to obtain maximum publicity for the Palestinian cause but was also designed to strain relations between the West German Government and Arab states in an effort to block peace proposals being initiated by Egypt through West Germany. The initiative was lost because Egypt refused to accede to the West German request to partake in the negotiations with the terrorists and as a result raised the ire of the West Germans. How one quantitatively assesses the passing of an opportunity for peace is unknown.

A similar curtailment of the public agenda can be observed in the motivations surrounding the assassination of Said Hammami, the representative of the Palestine Liberation Organization in London, who was shot to death on January 4, 1978 by a lone gunman believed to be acting for the hard-line Arab rejectionist front. Hammami, a political moderate, was involved in a continual dialogue with the Israelis in an effort to find a basis for negotiations between the PLO and Israel. His death, resulting in loss of his counsel and influence from PLO circles, makes more difficult and improbable PLO involvement in any dialogue that would ensue as a result of Egyptian President Anwar Sadat's visit to Israel. Certainly, those Arab extremists alleged to be responsible for Hammami's assassination believed that it would block the route to a more moderate course of action within the PLO. In the quantitative assessment of deaths attributed to terrorism, all are equal and equally anonymous. Hammami's death would carry no greater weight than that of any other anonymous victim of terrorist brutality.

Perhaps the most decisive attempt to affect the public agenda through terrorism occurred in March 1978 when a group of El Fatah terrorists, acting

under orders from PLO's Yassir Arafat, hijacked two
busloads of tourists north of Tel Aviv and began a
random attack on Israeli motorists. The incident
was timed to take place on the eve of Israeli Prime
Minster Begin's departure for Washington to discuss
the impasse that then existed in the talks begun as
a result of the Sadat initiative. The terrorists
hoped that the attack would harden the Israeli position and make negotiations more difficult. Moreover, it may have been Arafat's way of demonstrating
that moderation was not at all the position of the
PLO. No doubt the terrorists got more than they
bargained for as the Israelis decided that the
slaughter of some thirty innocents, half of them
children, was the last straw in a series of some one
thousand incidents launched from across the Leba-
nese border. Several days later the Israelis
launched a four-pronged assault into Fatah land, as
the region of Lebanon south of the Latani River has
become known. The long range implications of the
Israel incision into southern Lebanon are still
unknown. There is little doubt, however, that the
terrorists have made their impact on the public a-
genda.

IGNORING THE DOMESTIC CONSEQUENCES

    The implications for the United States from
such results are rather facilly dismissed as largely indirect and of minimal concern. This is especially the case when terrorism is commonly viewed
as a direct law enforcement problem, as it tends to
be within the Department of Justice, its subsidiary
agency, LEAA, and some law enforcement agencies.
It is also the position within the administration.
Terrorism is a problem that has, for the most part,
managed to confine itself beyond the domestic
boundaries and domestic policy concerns of the
United States.
    Such thinking of course fails to see terrorism
as an international phenomenon, one that has increasingly seen international cooperation as groups
provide one another with instruction, training
grounds, weapons, places of refuge, manpower for
one another's missions, and even the execution of
a mission in one another's behalf. The international cooperative aspects of terrorism are fur-
thered by nation states that direct and support
terrorist groups as instruments of foreign policy.
Such host nations as North Korea have brought to-

gether political radicals from across the globe,
to share information and ideologies, and to exchange
opportunities for mutual assistance. Members of the
Japanese Red army carried out a mission for the
Palestinians by massacring hapless tourists at Israel's Lod Airport. Basque separatists blew to bits
a high-ranking member of the Franco regime with a
bomb supplied by the Irish Republican Army. In
January 1974, British intelligence revealed that
Arab terrorists had agreed to cooperate with the IRA
in executing missions in Britain. In December 1973,
the French arrested thirteen suspected revolution-
aries, including Turks, Palestinians,and an Algerian. The Turks, members of the Popular Liberation Front of Turkey, had received their initiation
into the tactics of terrorism by Palestinians. The
West German Baader-Meinhof gang underwent training
by George Habash's Popular Front for the Liberation of Palestine. It was through the PFLP that
Baader-Meinhof developed ties with the Japanese Red
Army. In October 1977, a skyjacking by Baader-
Meinhof of a Lufthansa jet (that ended with the
daring raid by West German Commandos at Mogaidshu)
had, along with demands for the release of the 86
hostages, a demand for the release of two Palestinians in Turkish jails.

An unsuccessful attempt in January 1976 by members of the Popular Front for the Liberation of
Palestine to shoot down an El Al aircraft with sophisticated "heat seeking" missles is indicative of
the collusion between governments and terrorist
groups which serve as proxies for their foreign
policy endeavors. To this must be added the Entebbe
affair, the unleashing of a PLO assault team against
Egyptian commandos during the ill-fated Egyptian
raid at Lacarna, Cyprus,and the movement of Latin
American terrorist activity to Europe throught the
Revolutionary Coordinating Junta.

If the implications of transnational terrorist
cooperation for American security at home and a-
broad are difficult to discern, one might at least
be somewhat inspired to wrestle with the problem
by observing that the Central Intelligence Agency's
informative report on transnational terrorism notes
that in 1976 in"both relative and absolute terms,
the burden (from terrorist violence) born by U.S.
commercial facilities and their employees increased markedly over 1975."[8] The same statements
were as true in 1977 and 1978 as they were in
1976.[9]

The general tone of the CIA's "International

Terrorism in 1978" is that international terrorism
is getting worse. If the CIA's concern with international terrorism has any implications for domestic agencies, the relationship is difficult to
ferret out within the corridors of government. The
relative quiet of terrorist activity on the American domestic front is seen as confirmation for the
popular assertion in government circles that terrorism is not a serious problem for domestic concern. The general prognosis for domestic terrorism
is that the future is the present quietude, only
more so. Such thinking may well serve certain kinds
of policy functions, although it is unclear as to
what they are, but they may also leave us psychologically devastated when terrorism does rear its
ugly head on the American scene.

DR. KUPPERMAN: A VOICE IN THE WILDERNESS

One government official who is not very san-
guine about the future quietude of terrorism on the
domestic scene is Dr. Robert Kupperman, Chief
Scientist for the U.S. Arms Control and Disarmament
Agency. In a two-year study funded by LEAA, Kupperman[10] candidly describes some rather startling
but realistically threatening scenarios and concludes, "When we consider the abundance of targets
and cohesiveness of relatively small numbers of
well-trained zealots, the use of sophisticated
weaponry and the ease with which they could extort
governments, we are forced to ponder the future
with alarm."[11] In all probability Dr. Kupperman is
substantively correct. Unfortunately, within the
context of the current administration's perspective
on terrorism, he is not politically correct. Dr.
Kupperman is not very popular in government circles these days, having been referred to, in the
course of several recent conversations I have had
with government officials, as an "alarmist." That
designation is a most unfortunate one, and ultimately the misperception may affect all of us.
One of the most troubling aspects to Dr. Kupperman of the growing terrorist threat is the potential danger to society from biological and
chemical agents in terrorist hands. Not only can
chemical and biological weapons rival thermonuclear
weapons in their capacity to produce casualties,
but the knowledge and technical facilities required
to produce chemical and biological weapons are far
less esoteric than that required for thermonuclear

weapons. Moreover, the raw materials are far and
away more readily accessible. If such potential
scenarios sound as if they are alarmist, one might
consider than in 1975 Austrian authorities arrested
three erstwhile entrepreneurs who were synthesizing
nerve agents for sale to terrorist groups, and German terrorists have threatened to use mustard gas
against civilians. The validity of such threats
should be assessed in light of the growing affinity
between German terrorists and radicals in German
academic and scientific circles. The increased
coordination and cooperation between terrorist
groups can mean that materials and expertise obtained by one group could readily be made available
to other groups. Those decision makers in Washington who are sweeping aside the importance of the
current terrorist threat with pithy statements might
ponder Dr. Kupperman's position with greater concern and attention than has presently been mani-
fested.

POVERTY FROM SUCCESS

The unwillingness of the Carter administration
to conceive of terrorism as a serious threat stems
in small part from our success in countering certain types of terrorist operations. Our foremost
success has been in dealing with hostage and barricade situations. To effectively deal with these
situations, our police, especially in the large
cities, and the Federal Bureau of Investigation
have systematically put together a well-developed
tactical and psychological response. The success
of these procedures borders on the incredible. Although they have sustained only one test in this
country against political terrorists (during the
seizure in March, 1977 of hostages in three separate locations in Washington, D.C. by a band of
Hanafi Muslims), the procedures, when used against
armed and desperate men, often as desperate as any
band of terrorists and sometimes with far less to
lose, have been impressively successful. The
success of these procedures has brought police and
military observers from all over the Western world
to the Emergency Services Unit Headquarters of the
New York City Police Department. And even the Israelis, who in the face of a number of awesomely
difficult hostage situations persisted in the policy that is described in police and military circles as "surrender or die," have given pause to

consider the value of uniformly applying that policy in light of encounters by some of their people
with the lessons being taught in Brooklyn.

The procedures used by police and widely disseminated through training institutes run by the
NYPD and separately by the FBI build on the creation
of positive transference between hostage-taker and
victim. The catalyst is time. As the clock runs,
hostage-taker and hostage find themselves confined
to the same physical space and even the same fate.
With time comes intimacy, and intimacy acts as a
deterrent to killing. Except for moments of extreme anger, it is easier to kill a stranger than
someone one knows. With time comes ennui, dis-
traction, and a realization that the mission may
not be worth anyone's life. The taste of death
grows stale after one has gnawed on it for relent-
less hours.

The psychological drama is buttressed by highly
trained and exceptionally disciplines assault teams.
Their presence in full regalia -- heavy armaments,
flack jackets, and helmets -- adds its own dimensions to the drama. If talk fails, if negotiation
does not work, they are present to take over. That
message is not lost on the captors.

Assault teams seldom do take over. Most dramas
end because the psychological factors are adroitly
manipulated by the police with the assistance of
psychological professionals. The Hanafi Muslims
were not the first political terrorists to capitulate. The IRA has surrendered under similar circumstances to Scotland Yard (December 6, 1975),and
the first South Moluccan episode (December 2, 1975)
ended by capitulation; the second (May-June, 1977),
of course, did not.

SUCCESS MAY BE FLEETING

There is, however, no overall agreement on the
value of these techniques, and there is some concern that some terrorists are as astutely involved
in studying the hostage negotiation techniques that
have been developed to thwart them as we are involved in developing procedures to control the situation. In the first South Moluccan episode, one
of the terrorists attempted to build transference
by informing his Dutch captives that he could not
kill any of them because he was married to a Dutch
woman -- which of course he was not. By the second
South Moluccan episode, the terrorists had not only

studied the techniques of negotiation but also had
some knowledge of the negotiators and how they op-
erated. Dutch Psychiatrist Dick Mulder was greeted
in the course of initial contact with South Moluccan terrorist leader Max Papilaya with the quip,
"Oh, it's you Mulder."[12]

Although there is no monolithic hierarchy coordinating international terrorist activities, it
appears that there is a network of relationships
among terrorist groups where knowledge, information,
weaponry, and manpower are exchanged. As Claire
Sterling[13] has noted, terrorist groups such as West
Germany's Baader-Meinhof gang and Italy's Red Brigades have been linked with fellow terrorists in
the Middle East, Latin America,and Japan. In
fact, it was Argentina's Montoneros who first
brought together Renato Curico, of the Italian Red
Brigade, and Ulrike Meinhof, of the West German gang
which bore her name, at a secret meeting in Paris
in 1970. In the same year, links were formed between Baader-Meinhof and George Habash's Popular
Front for the Liberation of Palestine. Ulrike Meinhof, Andreas Baader,and Gudrun Enslin received
training in Jordan by the PFLP. This training continued throughout the seventies, with virtually
every known German terrorist receiving instruction
from camps run by George Habash or his associate
Wadi Haddad. The Red Brigades did not go to the
Middle East for training but to Czechoslovakia.
They did, however, receive assistance from the Palestinians who participated with them in the execution of missions.

Given that these exchanges do occur, as some
terrorist groups gain more sophistication and experience in dealing with the tactics of hostage
negotiation, it can be reasonably assumed that the
knowledge garnered by one group will be passed on
to another. One would then assume that the success
rate for negotiated capitulation might drop, or
terrorists and authorities might reach a standoff
in these scenarios with the terrorists, given their
penchant for safe targets, seeking other types of
activities. This does seem to be the case. The
CIA report on international terrorism for 1976
notes, "Risky and demanding kidnaping and barricade
and hostage situations declined, while the safest
and simplest types of terrorist action (bombing,
assassination, armed assault and incendiary attack)
registered sharp increases."[14] As these changes
occur, we can take less solace from our success
rates with hostage negotiations. Successful as

they have been in the past, they may be far less
important in the future, either because the terrorists will acquire a counter set of skills and procedures to ours or because of the already indicated
change in modus operandi. The use of counter tactics and strategies will necessitate an increased
reliance on armed assault. In those instances
the chances for spectacular success are as likely
as those for spectacular failure.

THE POLICY IMPLICATIONS OF COMPLACENCY

   Complacency about domestic terrorism is more
than just an attitude of mind. Invariably, this
attitude of mind is reflected in dozens of policy
choices across different levels of government.
Consequently, special weapons teams often operate
at the sufferance of city governments that perceive
them as exotic, unnecessary,and a superfluous drain
on the municipal budget. In some of our largest
cities, the marksmanship of special weapons units
is only maintained through the largess of cooperative National Guard commanders who illegally but
justifiably supply ammunition to local police to
enable them to maintain weapons proficiency.
   Where special weapons units do exist, their
equipment and training has been directed at dealing
with hostage and barricade situations perpetrated
by felons. These situations usually occur when a
felony is interrupted,and the perpetrators seize
hostages as a means to negotiate their freedom.
The original intent was not to take hostages. Unlike political terrorists, felons are neither mentally nor physically prepared for a long seige,
nor do they have any prospect of finding sanctuary
in the international community. The special weapons units and hostage negotiators are more than
adequately trained and prepared for this kind of
encounter, especially since the interrupted felon
is basically rational and appropriately recognizes
as time wears on that his hostages are more of a
liability than an asset. But in the one situation,
that involving the Hanafi Muslim attack in Washington, D.C., where police had to confront ideologically committed and prepared political terrorists,
the police found that they were terribly outgunned.
The two Uze submachine guns and auxiliary weapons
the police had were no match for the weaponry the
Hanafis brought into the B'nai B'rith Building. At
one point, there was discussion of an assault by

helicopter, but even if other conditions had fa-
vored such an operation, the assault team had never
been trained for this kind of operation. This is
far from an indictment of the D.C. barricade squad,
but an indication of our complacency about political
terrorism as a domestic issue. Fortunately, the
expertise of the D.C. police negotiators brought the
Hanafis to capitulation.

Aside from the absence of training and weaponry
to deal with the tactical situation mandated by
political terrorist operations, bureaucratic jealousies and the ambiguity of jurisdictional authority in our multi-layered system of government further contribute to the problems. In July 1974
a hostage situation in the U.S. Courthouse was,
because of overlapping jurisdictional control, run
by a committee with virtually every law enforcement
agency in Washington represented. Tactical responses often got bogged down in intra- and inter-
agency rivalries. At some points, freeing the hostages seemed almost secondary to the bureaucratic
conflict. A similar situation occurred in the
course of the skyjacking by Croatian separatists of
a TWA flight in September 1976. In the course of
making a decision about how to respond to the skyjackers' demands for an airdropping of leaflets demanding a free Croatia, the Federal Bureau of Investigation and the State Department parted company.
Attempts at resolution led to a clash over who was
actually in charge of the operation. The answer
was at best ambiguous.

As long as terrorism is not seen as a serious
domestic problem, resources will not be readily
available to counter terrorist activities, government agencies will find little impetus to get beyond interagency rivalries and jealousies, and
voices such as Dr. Kupperman's will echo in the
wind. In contrast to the reaction to terrorism
generally, domestic skyjacking has been taken seriously by government. In fact, it was the airline
industry that had opposed the creation of the now
commonplace surveillance equipment that has all but
eliminated skyjacking. The seriousness of government reaction put a quick end to jurisdictional
disputes arising between the FBI and the FAA over
decisions involving authority over skyjackings.
Their inter-agency agreement serves as a model for
other law enforcement agencies.

As a result of the success of the FBI and FAA
agreements, Memorandums of Understanding (MOUs)
have developed between the FAA and the Department

of Defense with regard to aircraft hijackings on
military bases; between FBI and the Department of
Energy on nuclear threat incidents; between DOE and
DOD on accidents or incidents involving radioactive
material or nuclear weapons; and between the Department of Justice and the Department of the Treasury
on bombing incidents.[15]

What must be appreciated about such matters is
not that agreements exist but how they work in
actual crisis situations. Inter-agency agreements,
like all legal-type instruments, are subject to
interpretation. Initially, such interpretations
may have to be made in crisis situations, not by
impartial jurists, but by administrative and operations personnel with differing bureaucratic interests and loyalties. The effectiveness of such
agreements will only fully be known through the
course of their implementation and the experiences
of real situations.

After an extensive review in 1977 by the National Security Council of the government's anti-terrorist effort, the State Department's Office for
Combating Terrorism was given what some, at least,
saw as an enhancing mandate to deal with both international and domestic terrorism, and what others saw
as bureaucratic reshuffling. The State Department
became the lead agency in terrorism activities involving international relations. Under guidance
of the Special Coordinating Committee of the National Security Council, the management of all terrorist
incidents is based on the lead agency concept, i.e.
an agency shall have major responsibility in its
given jurisdictional domain. But, in the past, the
scope of an agency's jurisdictional domain has been
open to serious dispute, a dispute confounded by
the somewhat unique overlay of multiple jurisdictions wrought by American federalism.

Prior to 1978, there was no mechanism for resolving inter-agency disputes except by taking the
case to the cabinet level, generally a politically
unwise and operationally impractical recourse. The
NSC review provides for the SCC to convene and resolve issues that cannot be resolved at the senior
official level. This type of mechanism for resolving disputes has been sorely needed; however, how
effective it will be remains to be seen. It focuses on the relationship between federal agencies
and hinges on a neatly packaged lead agency concept. Such delimiting does not always occur.
Often, the conflicts are between agencies, especially law enforcement agencies, operating at dif-

ferent levels of government. Beyond that, the delimiting of a situation, in clear enough terms for
there to be general agreement and understanding as
to which is the lead agency, also does not always
occur.

Sometimes the two problems, overlapping government jurisdictions and ambiguity about which federal agency is the lead agency, can occur simultaneously. Such a situation was hypothetically and
rather insightfully spelled out by Rep. Don Edwards
(California), Chairman of the Subcommittee on Civil
and Constitutional Rights of the House Committee on
the Judiciary. Rep. Edwards presented to Ambassador Anthony Quainton, Director, Office for Combating Terrorism, U.S. Department of State, a hypo-
thetical scenario describing a Yugoslav separatist
group taking over a dam owned by a state or public
utility. To this Ambassador Quainton responded:

> If I understand the situation almost all
> terrorist acts are also crimes under Federal
> statutes which would enable the FBI in
> consultation with the local law enforcement
> either to have concurrent jurisdiction or
> to agree which would be the appropriate
> jurisdiction. But they would certainly be
> immediately involved and would offer their
> services, as I understand it.[16]

It is not that simple. Almost all terrorism
acts are not federal crimes. Moreover, consultation with local law enforcement officials has, in
a number of cases, meant jurisdictional disagree-
ment. The situation Rep. Edwards described has at
least the potential to be fraught with jurisdictional difficulties.

The difficulties involved here were further
noted in the same hearings by Rep. M. Caldwell
Butler (Virginia). Rep. Butler posed the following
question to Ambassador Quainton: "What happens if
you lose the manual (referring to the delineation
of agencies responsible for different kinds of
activities)? We have several organization charts
which establish elaborate interagency communication. These things (referring to terrorist episodes) require quick action."[17]

The point is well taken. But the issue is even
more complex, for should the situation become
extremely serious it will fall into the hands of
the president and his advisors. And while that
solves Rep. Butler's concern about ultimate deci-

sion-making authority, it creates an additional
problem of some significance. What experience will
the president and his top-level advisors have to
deal with these situations?

What emerges, in part, from the government's
capability and response potential to terrorism is
a complicated series of relationships between
agencies exacerbated by the overlay of geographic
jurisdictions. Moreover, if a very serious episode occurs--however "serious" is defined--the
decision making may well be taken over by the president, and while this resolves the question of
ultimate decision-making authority, it certainly
does not put the most knowledgeable individual in
charge.

Too often, I have observed the consequences
when critical decisions passed from an operational
figure with expertise to a higher-ranking but
less knowledgeable authority. Not only was the
decision making less competent but, all too often,
political and public relations factors became para-
mount. In some cases the political and public relations issues became so important that it would
not be inaccurate to say that those issues took
on such significance that concern for the lives of
the hostages were lost as the focus of attention
shifted.

Obviously, it is easier to diagnose the illness
than to prescribe the cure. Some of the problems
are inherent, at least to some degree, in the
unique workings of our federal system. Since Ambassador Quainton stepped into office, there has
been a greater concern about these problems. Nonetheless, it is doubtful if the precise, decisive
response required in a major terrorist episode,
especially one brought about by political terrorists, would be forthcoming. The present system is
inordinately complicated. Rep. Butler's commentary
about the consequences of losing the agency manual
underscores this. The difficulties posed by com-
plexity are all the more poignant because terrorism
is still not viewed as a serious threat in many
corridors of the administration.

The kidnaping of former Italian premier Aldo
Moro in the wake of a series of other terrorist
activities in Europe prompted newly appointed FBI
Director William Webster to announce a new commitment within the Bureau to combat terrorism. One of
the most significant aspects of Webster's statement
was the admission that America could not forever
remain immune to or isolated from the current wave

of terrorism in Europe. However, before one becomes too enthusiastic about the emergence of a
new policy concern, it is best to keep in mind that
public pronouncements have precious little semblance
to agency policy. Bureaucratic attitudes and the
administration's orientation are not about to change
overnight. One of the most effective FBI anti-terrorist programs, the one involving hostage negotiations, was never a high status item within Bureau
circles because it produced no tallies for the Bureau's quantitative assessments of success--con-
victions. The program itself was largely funded by
LEAA, not the Bureau.[18] The seriousness of Webster's statements will be discerned from the resource commitment he is willing to make to such programs.

There is little doubt that once we incur the
direct experience of a devastating terrorist attack
there will be no end to the number of government
agencies which will react with concern, nor will we
be spared the flood of pious platitudes of commitment for which bureaucracies are known. However,
until such time, we will persist in the current
attitude of seeking to avoid taking any initiative
in a policy domain where the call to action appears
to be tantamount to alarmism. If the function of
this is to avoid public overreaction, those espousing such a policy should well consider how an un-
expecting public will react to an event that is
made all the more horrific because the government
itself was too ill-prepared to cope.

REFERENCES

1. For a discussion of the use of random
violence in the perpetration of state terrorism,
as distinct from terrorism used against the state
see: Hannah Arendt, The Origins of Totalitarianism
(New York: Meridian, 1971), esp. 419-437. The same
view is found in Carl J. Friedrich and Zbigniew K.
Brzezinski, Totalitarian Dictatorship and Autocracy
(New York: Frederick A. Praeger, 1968), esp. pp.
172-205.

2. The phrase is from the seminal work by
Harold D. Lasswell, Politics: Who Gets What, When
and How (New York: Meridian, 1958).

3. Ted Robert Gurr, Why Men Rebel (Princeton:
Princeton University Press, 1971), p. 237.

4. From interviews with high-ranking officials
of the New York Police Department.

5.   From interviews with government personnel involved in anti-terrorist measures.

6.   Jacob K. Javits, "International Terrorism: Apathy Exacerbates the Problem," Terrorism: An International Journal, 1,2, (1978) p. 112.

7.   Ibid., p. 115.

8.   International Terrorism in 1976 (Washington, D.C.: Central Intelligence Agency, 1977).

9.   International Terrorism in 1977 (Washington, D.C.: Central Intelligence Agency, 1978). International Terrorism in 1978 (Washington, D.C.: Central Intelligence Agency, 1979).

10.   Robert H. Kupperman, Facing Tomorrow's Terrorist Incident Today (Washington, D.C.: Law Enforcement Assistance Administration, 1977).

11.   Ibid., p. 4.

12.   "Psyching Out Terrorists," Medical World News, (June 27, 1977).

13.   Claire Sterling, "The Terrorist Network," The Atlantic 242, 5, (November, 1978), p. 41.

14.   International Terrorism in 1976, op. cit., p. 2.

15.   Testimony of Ambassador Anthony Quainton, Hearings, Subcommittee on Civil and Constitutional Rights of the Committee on the Judiciary, House of Representatives, Ninety-fifth Congress, Second Session, Federal Capabilities in Crisis Management and Terrorism, Serial No. 77 (Washington, D.C.: U.S. Government Printing Office, 1978).

16.   Ibid., p. 49.

17.   Ibid.

18.   Testimony of Perry A. Rivkind, Ibid., p. 740.

7
Conclusion

The conclusions arrived at here must be viewed in
terms of the caveats expressed. Access to information about some terrorist episodes was extensive,
while on others it was minimal. Without coverage of
the foreign language press, a task far in excess of
this undertaking, and without corresponding details
from officials who were involved in the whole range
of specific episodes, an unobtainable commodity because of resource and security considerations, the
exposure to the universe of existent information is
limited. The inferences made, conclusions drawn,
and policies recommended are of necessity shaped by
one's exposure to information, and the extent to
which any of this is representative of the universe
of information is unknown. The expression of such
qualifications is not to detract from the findings
but to place them in a perspective mandated by legitimate concerns for objective scholarship. Consequently, given the ever-changing nature of terrorist operations, and the considerations expressed a-
bove, scholars and decision makers will have to assess the observations drawn from this research in
light of those caveats and their own experiences--
recalling all the time that every hostage situation
and terrorist operation, in addition to its general
aspects, contains unique situational considerations.
The application of any general guidelines must be
weighed against the unique aspects of a given situation.

With such qualification, let us observe the conclusions of this research.

1. Hostage negotiations require a coordinated
   set of predetermined tactics between special
   weapons units and trained negotiators, who
   may or may not be located within the special

113

weapons unit. Negotiation is an extension of police work. It is not a substitute for it. It is not a business to be left to those who are not specially trained, irrespective of years of experience or rank.

2. The application of negotiation techniques has been most successful in situations involving interrupted felonies. Felons are basically rational, do not intend initially to take hostages, and soon comprehend that by holding on to their hostages they only increase the likelihood of their own death or a long and difficult prison term. The problem generally in getting felons to capitulate is to convince them that the heavily armed special weapons team will not be unleashed against them if they surrender.

3. The tactics used in hostage and barricade situations with felons have some likelihood of success in situations involving political terrorists, if the terrorists are primarily interested in making a symbolic statement and obtaining an otherwise unachievable amount of publicity. In such situations, deference to the terrorists on symbolic issues can lead to their capitulation. The question, of course, is whether or not symbolic concerns and symbolic rewards are sufficient. In the Hanafi Muslim episode this was the case; however, applying generalizations to such groups as the Italian Red Brigade, the Japanese Red Army and the Baader-Meinhof gang raises serious questions, although one must consider that members of the Irish Republican Army and the Black September Organization have on occasion capitulated. If the prospect of sanctuary can be eliminated, the behavior of political terrorists will probably not be different from that of convicts, who frequently capitulate to negotiation techniques. It should also be kept in mind that contrary to common perception, few political terrorist missions are suicidal in character. Most involve very elaborate escape plans.

4. An open policy of nonnegotiation will most likely not act as a deterrent to political hostage taking. Since such a policy does not appear to act as a deterrent and seems to have secondary consequences, such as

creating morale problems among our overseas
personnel, the wisdom of such a policy is
questionable. If the observations from this
research are correct, to the effect that
some political hostage taking is undertaken
solely for symbolic purposes,then a pre-an-
nounced position of nonnegotiation precludes using the range of options open in
such a situation. Could the Hanafi Muslim
episode have been brought to a successful
conclusion if the option of negotiation had
been precluded or if our domestic police had
been required to adhere to our external policy of nonnegotiation?

5. Because we note that a policy of nonnegotiation will not deter terrorists does not mean
that we are advocating a soft line. This is
hardly the case. Evidence indicates that
the policy of nonnegotiation not only fails
to act a a deterrent but creates morale
problems among our overseas personnel. Consequently, it does not appear functional.
Even the Israelis, whose toughness in such
matter is well known, do not advertise their
negotiation policy in advance.

6. Irrespective of policy, certain governments
and their citizens are going to be targets
because of reasons relevant to the terrorists' perception of their struggle. Whether a hard line acts as a <u>significant</u> deterrent in such cases is questionable. Few,
however, will argue that a soft approach
does not invite difficulties. Moreover,
consideration must be given to what policy
is employed for what type of terrorist behavior. Meeting force with force, harden-
ing targets, and handing down stiff sentences are more functional responses than
the policy of nonnegotiation has been. Israeli intelligence indicates that when terrorist groups suffer heavy casualties upon
executing raids in Israel, it is difficult
for them to recruit for the next raid.

7. The type of policy a government will be able
to implement in dealing with terrorists is
a function of the political climate a government confronts. West Germany, for example, was able to move to a tougher policy
after it gained support as a result of public outrage in response to the kidnaping of
CDU mayoral candidate Peter Lorenz. Since

Mogadishu and the ensuing series of outrages committed by Baader-Meinhof, West Germany has strong public support for a hard line. At the same time, a government must not simply react to public opinion but exert its leadership. Governments must not so revise their democratic codes of behavior as to achieve for the terrorists what they cannot achieve for themselves.

8. Hostage negotiators have talked about time being on the side of the negotiator in barricade and hostage situations. This is true when a process of mutual identification, sometimes referred to as "psychological transference," takes place between hostage and captor. With time comes intimacy and as a result the captor is less likely to kill his captive. Transference, however, has a higher probability of being asymmetically a hostage reaction. (In fact, either way, the effect of transference is such as to preclude negotiators from trusting hostages.) As terrorists, such as the South Moluccans, study hostage negotiations, transference can be manipulated by the terrorists to control the hostages. Consequently, techniques that currently work because of the negotiators' ability to manipulate the transference between hostage and hostage taker might not work in the future.

9. Transference is not a simple function of time but a result of the influence of a number of variables. In addition to time, these are:
   1. The quality of interaction, e.g., were the hostages well treated?
   2. The existence of predetermined racial or ethnic hostilities between captive and captor.
   3. The predisposition on the part of some hostages to initiate relationships with their captors.

10. The scenario of hostage negotiations has three basic elements which determine their likely outcome:
    1. Who are the hostage takers and what are their motives?
    2. Who are the hostages?
    3. What demands are being made and on whom?

11. The experience of being a hostage does not end with the resolution of the situation.

Hostages often experience long periods of suffering and some governments, such as Israel and the Netherlands, have devoted government resources to help alleviate the plight of hostages.

12. The long-term effects of a lengthy exposure to stress during captivity have become concerns that have led to reexamining the wisdom of throwing away the clock, waiting out the terrorists. Questions have ensued about not only saving lives but the quality of the lives saved.

13. It is possible for individuals who are likely to be taken hostage to prepare themselves for captivity and interrogation. The experiences of Dr. Claude Fry, an American agronomist, and Sir Geoffrey Jackson, the former British Ambassador to Uruguay, are instructive in this matter. Both men were better able to handle their captivity because they had mentally prepared themselves for it. The most crucial thing that preparation accomplishes is the reduction of anxiety caused by uncertainty and ambiguity.

14. One of the critical and most controversial issues facing negotiating units within domestic police departments is whether or not negotiators should be independent of or part of the special weapons unit. Problems exist no matter which choice is made. If the negotiators are part of the team their orientation as negotiators as well as the direction of their training for that role may be compromised. If negotiators are not part of the team, then conflicts and communications difficulties can arise between negotiators and team members. The means to avoid this is to require joint debriefings between special weapons personnel and negotiators.

15. Since a special weapons team will be an elite unit, its existence will incur jealousies within a department. One way to avoid some of these problems is not to provide extra pay and to restrict the special units from making arrests.

16. Training procedures and recruitment for SWAT teams vary widely, with different emphases on different levels of physical conditioning. One of the most demanding physical programs is that conducted by the Chicago

Police Department for its team. The Chicago program is worthy of emulation for any department that believes that a special weapons team requires special physical preparedness.

17. Specialized training sessions, like those conducted by the FBI for police departments in the San Francisco Bay Area, play a vital role in assisting with departmental cooperation when called for and preparing units for the potentially difficult problems which they will be called upon to face.

18. Special weapons teams face a series of unique problems. Some of these emanate from the drama surrounding their operations. Other law enforcement personnel and politicians want all too frequently to maximize publicity from special weapons operations, causing interference with the tactical procedures and placing commanders in the difficult and precarious situation of being heroes if they succees and failures if they do not. Too frequently, the same politicians who wish to stand in the afterglow of a successful operation perceive the entire concept as a fad when it comes to supporting appropriations for the unit.

19. Terrorism in many of its forms is an attempt to gain access to the public agenda and consequently access to the media. It is for this reason that guerrilla warfare moved from an area of little exposure, the countryside, to an area of high exposure, the city.

20. Terrorists seek to maximize exposure, and, as a result, the choice of target and operation may be predicted on whether or not it will serve as a good media event, especially as a good visual media event.

21. Because terrorists need public exposure, the often unwitting support of the media in terrorist activities places a special obligation on the media. Unfortunately, until very recently, few media sources have demonstrated any concern over this special relationship.

22. Although it is easy to articulate the problem presented by the manipulation of the media by terrorists and the media's hunger for spectacle, it is difficult to find a solution, other than espousing a

conscientious and ethical self-restraint.
Censorship is ill-advised. What one source
ignores, another will report. Censorship--
even if legally possible--would only cause
the terrorists to further escalate the prominence of their targets.

23. In addition to the question of what the media reports, there is the issue of how they
report it. Some believe that the media has
generally presented the terrorists on their
own terms and given them very favorable coverage.

24. One of the most frequent complaints of the
police concerns the intrusion of media people in the police operation. Sometimes this
has been so callously done as to have jeopardized lives. Here, the balance between
the public's right to know and the captives'
rights to survive must tilt in favor of the
captives.

25. If a capricious, callous, and unthinking media becomes so wrapped up in its pursuit of
sensational copy that it will violate the
public trust, it will become vulnerable to
public clamor for censorship.

26. In direct contrast to government policy toward international terrorism, government
policy toward domestic terrorism, as an actual or potential threat or even as a function of international terrorism, has been
largely one of ignoring domestic terrorism.

27. This policy ensues from a rigid view of the
costs of terrorism as a domestic problem,
a view which fails to consider both the symbolic implications of terrorism or the potential relationship between international
and domestic terrorism.

28. The policy implications of this type of
complacency have been to ignore some of the
current problems confronting our domestic
anti-terrorist operations, most noteworthy
in the domain of inter-agency jurisdictional
disputes. Unfortunately, it will probably
take a domestic terrorist incident of substantial proportions to shock us into per-
ceiving terrorism as a significant domestic
problem.

Bibliography

Alexander, Yonah, ed., International Terrorism: National, Regional, and Global Perspectives (New York: Praeger, 1976).

Alexander, Yonah, Carlton, David, and Wilkinson, Paul, eds., Terrorism: Theory and Practice (Boulder, Colorado: Westview Press, 1979).

Alexander, Yonah and Kilmarx, Robert A., eds., Political Terrorism and Business: The Threat and Response (New York: Praeger, 1979).

Alves, Marcio Moreira. A Grain of Mustard Seed: The Awakening of the Brazilian Revolution (Garden City, New York: Doubleday Anchor, 1973).

Arendt, Hannah. The Origins of Totalitarianism (New York: Meridian, 1962).

Austria, Federal Chancellory. "The Events of September 28 and 29, 1973: A Documentary Report," (Vienna, 1973).

Becker, Jillian. Hitler's Children: The Story of the Baader-Meinhof Gang (London: Granada Publishing, 1978).

Begin, Menachem. The Revolt (New York: Henry Schumer, 1951).

Bell, J. Bowyer. "Assassination in International Politics: Lord Moyne, Count Bernadotte and the Lehi," 16, 1 International Studies Quarterly (March 1972), pp. 59-82.

Bell, J. Bowyer. On Revolt: Strategies of National Liberation (Cambridge, Massachusetts: Harvard University Press, 1976).

Bell, J. Bowyer. A Time of Terror (New York: Basic Books, 1978).

Bell, J. Bowyer. Transnational Terror (Stanford and Washington: Hoover Institution and American Enterprise Institute, 1975).

Bell, Robert G. "The U.S. Response to Terrorism Against International Civil Aviation," Orbis 19, 4 (Winter 1976), pp. 1326-1343.

Belz, Mary, et al. "Is There A Treatment for Terror?", Psychology Today (October 1977), pp. 54-56; 108-112.

Brockman, Richard. "Notes While Being Hijacked," The Atlantic (December 1976).

Brower, Charles N. "Aircraft Hijacking and Sabotage: Initiative or Inertia?", Department of State Bulletin, 68 (June 18, 1973), pp. 872-875.

Carlton, David and Schaerf, Carlo, eds., International Terrorism and World Security (New York: The Halsted Press, 1975).

Cawley, Donald F. "Anatomy of a Siege," The Police Chief (January 1974).

Central Intelligence Agency. International Terrorism in 1976 (Washington, D.C.: Central Intelligence Agency, 1977).

Central Intelligence Agency. International Terrorism in 1977 (Washington, D.C.: Central Intelligence Agency, 1978).

Central Intelligence Agency. International Terrorism in 1978 (Washington, D.C.: Central Intelligence Agency, 1979).

Clines, Thomas G. "The Urban Insurgents" (Newport, Rhode Island: Naval War College, 1972).

Clutterbuck, Richard. Protest and the Urban Guerrilla (London: Abelard-Schuman, 1973).

Cooper, H.H.A. "Terrorism and the Media," in Yonah Alexander and Seymour Maxwell Finger, eds., Terrorism: Interdisciplinary Perspectives (New York: John Jay Press, 1977).

Craib, Ralph. "Crisis Negotiators in Hostage Cases," The San Francisco Chronicle (January 29, 1977), p. 2.

Crozier, Brian. The Rebels: A Study of Post-War Insurrections (Boston, Massachusetts: Beacon Press, 1960).

Culley, Lt. John A. "Defusing Human Bombs--Hostage Negotiations," FBI Law Enforcement Bulletin (October 1974), pp. 10-14.

Dobson, Christopher. Black September: Its Short, Violent History (New York: Macmillan, 1974).

Dortzbach, Karl and Debbie. Kidnapped (New York: Harper and Row, 1975).

Elliot, Major John D. "Action and Reaction: West Germany and the Baader-Meinhof Guerrillas," Strategic Review, IV, 1 (Winter 1976), pp. 31-60.

Elliott, Major John D. "Primers on Terrorism,"
    Military Review (October 1976).

Etinger, Leo. Concentration Camp Survivors in Norway
    and Israel (London: Allen and Unwin, 1964).

Evans, Alona E. "Aircraft Hijacking," American
    Journal of International Law 67, 4 (October 1973)
    pp. 641-671.

Fearey, Robert A. "International Terrorism," Depart-
    ment of State Bulletin (March 29, 1976).

Feierabend, Ivo K., and others, "Social Changes and
    Political Violence: Cross-National Patterns,"
    in Hugh Davis Graham and Ted Robert Gurr, eds.,
    The History of Violence in America (New York:
    Bantam Books, 1970).

Fenyvesi, C. "Looking into the Muzzle of Terrorists,"
    The Quill, 1977, pp. 16-18.

Fly, Claude. No Hope But God (New York: Hawthorn
    Books, Inc., 1973).

Fromkin, David. "The Strategy of Terrorism," For-
    eign Affairs, 53, 4 (July 1975), pp. 683-698.

Friedlander, Robert A. "Coping with Terrorism: What
    Is To Be Done?" in Yonah Alexander, David Carl-
    ton and Paul Wilkinson, eds., Terrorism: Theory
    and Practice (Boulder, Colorado: Westview Press,
    1979).

Friedlander, Robert A., ed.,Terrorism: Documents of
    International and Local Control (Dobbs Ferry,
    New York: Oceana, 1979) 2 vols.

Friedlander, Robert A. "The Origins of International
    Terrorism: A Micro Legal-Historical Perspec-
    tive," Israel Yearbook on Human Rights, V6
    (Tel Aviv: Faculty of Law, Tel Aviv University,
    1976).

Friedlander, Robert A. "Reflections on Terrorist
    Havens," Naval War College Review 32, 2 (March-
    April 1979), pp. 59-67.

Friedlander, Robert A. "Sowing The Wind: Rebellion
    and Terror-Violence in Theory and Practice,"
    Denver Journal of International Law and Policy,
    6, 1 (Spring 1976), pp. 83-93.

Friedlander, Robert A. "Terrorism and Political
    Violence: Do The Ends Justify The Means,"
    Chitty's Law Journal (Canada) 24,7 (September
    1976), pp. 240-246.

Friedrich, Carl J. and Brzezinski, Zbigniew K.
    Totalitarian Dictatorship and Autocracy (New
    York: Praeger, 1968).

Gaucher, Roland, Les Terroristes (Paris: Albin
    Michel, 1965); English Translation, The Terror-
    ists: From Tsarist Russia to the OAS (London:
    Secker and Warburg, 1968).

Giap, Vo Nguyen, People's War, People's Army (New York: Praeger, 1967).

Goodspeed, D.J. The Conspirators: A Study of Coup d'Etat (Toronto: Macmillan, 1967).

Green, L.C. "Humanitarian Intervention-1976 Version," Chitty's Law Journal, 24, 7 (September 1976), pp. 217-225.

Grivas, General George. Guerrilla Warfare and EOKA's Struggle (London: Longmans, 1964).

Gurr, Ted Robert. Why Men Rebel (Princeton: Princeton University Press, 1971).

Hamburg, David A., and Adams John E. "A Perspective on Coping Behavior," Archives of General Psychiatry 17 (1967).

Hassel, Conrad V. "Terror: The Crime of the Priviledged-An Examination and Prognosis," Terrorism: An International Journal, 1, 1 (1977), pp. 1-16.

Hickey, Neil. "Terrorism and Television," Part 1, TV Guide (July 31, August 6, 1976), pp. 2-6.

Hickey, Neil. "Terrorism and Television: The Medium in the Middle," Part 2, TV Guide (August 7-13, 1976), pp. 10-13.

Hodges, Donald C. Philosophy of the Urban Guerrilla, The Revolutionary Writings of Abraham Guillen (New York: William Morrow and Company, 1973).

Hoffer, Eric. The True Believer (New York: Mentor, 1958).

Howard, Bruce. "Living With Terrorism," Washington Post (July 18, 1976), pp. C-1, C-4.

Hubbard, David. "The Terrorist Mind," Counterforce (April 1971), pp. 12-13.

Hussaini, Hatem I., and Fathalla El-Boghdady, eds., The Palestinians: Selected Essays (Washington, D.C.: Arab Information Center, 1976).

Hutchinson, Martha C. "The Concept of Revolutionary Terrorism," Journal of Conflict Resolution, 16, 3 (September 1972), pp. 383-396.

Jackson, Geoffrey. Surviving the Long Night: An Autobiographical Account of a Political Kidnapping (New York: Vanguard, 1974).

Jackson, Robert J., and others. "Collective Conflict, Violence and the Media in Canada," (Ottawa: Carleton University, unpublished).

Javits, Jacob K. "International Terrorism: Apathy Exacerbates the Problem," Terrorism: An International Journal, 1, 2 (1978), pp. 111-117.

Jenkins, Brian M. "High Technology Terrorism and Surrogate War: The Impact of New Technology on Low-Level Violence," (Santa Monica: RAND Corporation, P-5339, January 1975).

Jenkins, Brian M. "Hostage Survival: Some Prelimi-
    nary Observations," (Santa Monica: RAND Corpor-
    ation, P-5627, April 1976).
Jenkins, Brian M. "International Terrorism: A New
    Kind of Warfare," (Santa Monica: The RAND Cor-
    poration, P-5261, June 1974).
Jenkins, Brian M. "International Terrorism: A New
    Mode of Conflict," in David Carlton and Carlo
    Schaerf, eds., International Terrorism and World
    Security (New York: The Halsted Press, 1975).
Jenkins, Brian M., and others. "Numbered Lives: Some
    Statistical Observations From Seventy-Seven In-
    ternational Hostage Episodes, " (Santa Monica:
    RAND Corporation, 1977).
Jenkins, Brian M. "Terrorism Works--Sometimes,"
    (Santa Monica: RAND Corporation, P-5217, April
    1974).
Jones, Juanita B., and Miller, Abraham H. "Terrorism
    and the Media: Resolving the First Amendment
    Dilemma," Ohio Northern University Law Review,
    forthcoming.
Kaplan, John. "The Assassins," Stanford Law Review,
    19, 5 (May 1967), pp. 1110-1151.
Kirkham, James F., Levy, Sheldon G., and Crotty,
    William J. Assassination and Political Violence:
    A Staff Report to the National Commission on the
    Causes and Prevention of Violence (New York:
    Bantam, 1970).
Kissinger, Henry A. "Hijacking, Terrorism and War,"
    Department of State Bulletin, 73 (September 8,
    1975), pp. 360-361.
Kupperman, Robert H. Facing Tomorrow's Terrorist
    Incident Today (Washington, D.C.: Law Enforce-
    ment Assistance Administration, 1977).
Lacqueur, Walter. "The Futility of Terrorism,"
    Harpers (March 1976), pp. 99-105.
Lacqueur, Walter. Terrorism (London: Abacus, 1977).
Lacqueur, Walter. The Terrorism Reader (Philadel-
    phia: Temple University Press, 1978).
Lafflin, John. Fedayeen (Glencoe: The Free Press,
    1973).
Lang, Daniel, "A Reporter at Large: The Bank Drama,"
    New Yorker Magazine (November 25, 1974), pp. 56-
    126.
Lasky, Melvin J. "Ulrike Meinhof and the Baader-
    Meinhof Gang," Encounter, 44 (June 1975), pp.15-
    16.
Lasswell, Harold D. Politics: Who Gets What, When,
    and How (New York: Meridian, 1958).
Leiden, Carl. "Assassination in the Middle East,"
    Trans-Action 6 (May 1969) pp. 20-23.

Mallin, Jay. "Terrorism in Revolutionary Warfare," Strategic Review (Fall 1974), pp. 48-55.

McEvoy, James and Miller Abraham H. "On Strike Shut It Down...The Crisis at San Francisco State College," Trans-Action 6 (March 1969), pp. 18-23; 61-62.

Medical World News. "Psyching Out Terrorists," (June 27, 1977).

Mickolus, Edward. Codebook: ITERATE (Ann Arbor: Inter-University Consortium for Political and Social Research, University of Michigan, 1976).

Mickolus, Edward. "Negotiating For Hostages: A Policy Dilemma," 19, 4 Orbis (Winter 1976), pp. 1309-1325.

Mickolus, Edward. "Statistical Approaches to the Study of Terrorism," in Yonah Alexander and Seymour Maxwell Finger, eds., Terrorism: Interdisciplinary Perspectives (New York: John Jay Press, 1977).

Milbank, David L. Research Study: International and Transnational Terrorism: Diagnosis and Prognosis (Washington, D.C: Central Intelligence Agency, PR7610030, April 1976).

Miller, Abraham H. "Negotiations For Hostages: Implications From the Police Experience," Terrorism: An International Journal 1, 2 (1978).

Miller, Abraham H. "On Terrorism," Public Administration Review, 37, 4 (July/August 1977), pp. 429-434.

Miller, Abraham H. "People's Park: Dimensions of a Campus Confrontation," Politics and Society, 2 (Summer 1972), pp. 433-455.

Miller, Abraham H., and others. "The J-Curve Theory and the Black Urban Riots," The American Political Science Review, 71, 3 (September 1977), pp. 964-982.

Miller, Abraham H., and others. "The New Urban Blacks," Ethnicity 3 (December 1976), pp. 338-367.

Moss, Robert. The War for the Cities (New York: Coward, McCann, and Geoghegan, 1972).

Ochberg, Frank. "The Victim of Terrorism: Psychiatric Considerations," Terrorism: An International Journal, 1, 2 (1978), pp. 147-168.

Oren, Uri. Ninety-nine Days in Damascus: The Story of Professor Shlomo Samueloff and the Hijack of TWA Flight 840 to Damascus (London: Weidenfeld and Nicholson, 1970).

Plastrik, S. "On Terrorism," Dissent 21 (Spring 1974).

Rapoport, David C. Assassination and Terrorism
     (Toronto: Canadian Broadcasting Corporation,
     1971).
Rogers, William P. "US and Cuba Reach Agreement on
     Hijacking," Department of State Bulletin 69
     (September 10, 1972), pp. 356-358.
Romaniecki, Leon. "The Soviet Union and Internation-
     al Terrorism," Soviet Studies 24, 3 (July 1974).
Russel, Charles A., Banker, Leon J., Jr., and
     Miller, Bowman H., "Out-Inventing The Terror-
     ist," in Yonah Alexander, David Carlton and
     Paul Wilkinson, eds., Terrorism: Theory and Prac-
     tice (Boulder, Colorado: Westview Press, 1979).
Schein, E.H., and others. "Distinguishing Charac-
     teristics of Collaborators and Resisters Among
     American Prisoners of War," The Journal of Ab-
     normal Social Psychology 55 (1957) pp. 197-201.
Shimbori, Michiya. "The Sociology of a Student Move-
     ment--A Japanese Case Study," Daedalus (Winter
     1968).
Singh, Baljit. "Political Terrorism: Some Third
     World Perspectives," paper presented to the XVII
     Annual Convention of the International Studies
     Association, March 16, 1977, St. Louis, Missou-
     ri.
Sloan, Stephen. "Simulating Terrorism: From Opera-
     tional Techniques To Questions of Policy,"
     International Studies Notes (Winter 1978), pp.
     3-8.
Sobel, Lester A., ed., Political Terrorism (New York:
     Facts on File, Inc., 1975).
Sterling, Claire. "The Terrorist Network," The At-
     lantic 242, 5 (November 1978), pp. 37-47.
Stevenson, William. Ninety Minutes at Entebbe (New
     York: Bantam, 1976).
Stewart, M. Jane. "Hostage Episodes, 1973-1977: A
     Chronology," (Unpublished).
Thornton, Thomas Perry. "Terror as a Weapon of Po-
     litical Agitation," in Harry Eckstein, ed.,
     Internal War Problems and Approaches (New York:
     The Free Press, 1964).
US Department of Justice. Law Enforcement Assistance
     Administration, Task Force on Disorders and Ter-
     rorism, Disorders and Terrorism (Washington,
     D.C.: LEAA, 1976).
US Department of Justice. Terrorist Activities:
     Bibliography (Quantico, Virginia: FBI Academy,
     1975).
US Department of State. Background Documentation
     Relating to the Assassinations of Ambassador
     Cleo A. Noel, Jr. and George Curtis Moore

(Washington, D.C.: US Department of State, 1973).

US House of Representatives. Committee on Foreign Affairs, Subcommittee on the Near East and South Asia, "International Terrorism: Hearings," Ninety-Third Congress, Second Session, June 11-24, 1974 (Washington, D.C.: US Government Printing Office, 1974).

US House of Representatives. Committee on the Judiciary, Subcommittee on Civil and Constitutional Rights, "Federal Capabilities in Crisis Management and Terrorism: Hearings," Ninety-Fifth Congress, Second Session, August 16, September 15-28, and October 4, 1978 (Washington, D.C.: US Government Printing Office, 1978).

US House of Representatives. Committee on Internal Security, The Symbionese Liberation Army: A Study, Ninety-Third Congress, Second Session (Washington, D.C.: US Government Printing Office, 1974).

US House of Representatives. Committee on Internal Security, Terrorism: A Staff Study, Ninety-Third Congress, Second Session, August 1, 1974 (Washington, D.C.: US Government Printing Office, 1974).

US House of Representatives. Committee on Internal Security, "Terrorism: Hearings," Parts 1-4, Ninety-Third Congress, Second Session, February-August 1974 Washington, D.C.: US Government Printing Office, 1974)

US Senate. Committee on the Judiciary, Subcommittee on Criminal Laws and Procedures, "The Terrorist and His Victim: Hearing," Ninety-Fifth Congress, First Session, July 21, 1977 (Washington, D.C.: US Government Printing Office, 1977).

US Senate. Committee on the Judiciary, Subcommittee to Investigate the Administration of the Internal Security Act and Other Security Laws, "Terroristic Activity: Hearings," Part 1, Ninety-Third Congress, Second Session, September 23, 1974 (Washington, D.C.: US Government Printing Office, 1974).

US Senate. Committee on the Judiciary, Subcommittee to Investigate the Administration of the Internal Security Act and Other Internal Security Laws, "Terroristic Activity, Hostage Defense Measures: Hearings," Part 5, Ninety-Fourth Congress, First Session, July 25, 1975, (Washington, D.C.: US Government Printing Office, 1975).

US Senate. Committee on the Judiciary, Subcommittee
    to Investigate the Administration of the In-
    ternal Security Act and Other Internal Security
    Laws," Terroristic Activity, Inside the Weather-
    man Movement: Hearings," Part 2, Ninety-Third
    Congress, Second Session, October 18, 1974
    (Washington, D.C.: US Government Printing Of-
    fice, 1975).
US Senate. Committee on the Judiciary, Subcommittee
    to Investigate the Administration of the In-
    ternal Security Act and Other Internal Security
    Laws, "Terroristic Activity, International Ter-
    rorism: Hearings," Part 4, Ninety-Fourth Con-
    gress, First Session, May 14, 1975 (Washington,
    D.C.: US Government Printing Office, 1975).
US Senate. Committee on the Judiciary, Subcommittee
    to Investigate the Administration of the In-
    ternal Security Act and Other Security Laws,
    The Weather Underground: Report, Ninety-Third
    Congress, Second Session (Washington, D.C.:
    US Government Printing Office, 1975).
Walter, Eugene Victor. "Violence and the Process
    of Terror," American Sociological Review 29,
    (April 1964), pp. 248-257.
Wilkinson, Paul. Political Terrorism (New York:
    Halsted Press, 1975).
Wilkinson, Paul. Terrorism and the Liberal State
    (London: Macmillan Press Ltd., 1977).
Wilkinson, Paul. "Three Questions of Terrorism,"
    Government and Opposition, 8, 3 (Summer 1975),
    pp. 290-312.
Wilson, Colin. Order of Assassins: The Psychology
    of Murder (London: Rupert Hart-Davis, 1972).
Winegarten, Renee. "Literary Terrorism," Commentary,
    57 (March 1974), pp. 58-65.

Index